Love Magic

Love Magic

A Book of Spells to Solve Every Relationship Problem You've Ever Had

Sheryn George

CITADEL PRESS
Kensington Publishing Corp.
www.kensingtonbooks.com

While the author has researched the recipes and spells in this book, ingredients can vary, especially the active ingredients of herbs. Conditions under which the recipies are made may differ, or the products might be used in ways the author could not have anticipated. The author and publishers cannot accept responsibility for any adverse health effects or undiscovered hazards of foods or herbs or essential oils, or for any injuries, losses or other damages that may result from the use of the information in this book.

A note on essential oils.
Some essential oils can be harmful. Please take note of the following points: never apply essential oils directly on your skin, never take essential oils internally, discontinue the use of essential oils immediately if you suffer an allergic reaction, and seek porifessional advice; never dilute more than a total of eight drops of essential oils in water for vaporization, unless advised otherwise by a qualified aromatherapist or naturopath; if you are pregnant (or there is a chance you are pregnant) consult a qualified aromatherapist, naturopath, or your family doctor, before using any essential oil; keep oils out of reach of children.

CITADEL PRESS BOOKS are published by

Kensington Publishing Corp.
850 Third Avenue
New York, NY 10022

Copyright © 2002 Sheryn George

All rights reserved. No part of this book may be reproduced in any form or by any means without the prior written consent of the publisher, excepting brief quotes used in reviews.

All Kensington titles, imprints, and distributed lines are available at special quantity discounts for bulk purchases for sales promotions, premiums, fund-raising, educational, or institutional use. Special book excerpts or customized printings can also be created to fit specific needs. For details, write or phone the office of the Kensington special sales manager: Kensington Publishing Corp., 850 Third Avenue, New York, NY 10022, attn: Special Sales Department; phone 1-800-221-2647.

CITADEL PRESS and the Citadel logo are Reg. U.S. Pat. & TM Off.

First Citadel printing: January 2004

10 9 8 7 6 5 4 3 2 1

Printed in the United States of America

Library of Congress Control Number: 2003109697

ISBN 0-8065-2594-0

For Thomasina

Contents

Introduction		1
1	*The essentials of spellcasting*	7
	(How to use magic and spells)	
2	*Why isn't he here yet?*	37
	(The lament of the single girl)	
3	*A few good men: Location, location, location*	45
	(Or, where men materialize these days)	
4	*Did I just meet Mr. Right?*	55
	(How to recognize a hot prospect from a not prospect)	
5	*First date trauma*	63
	(Have you got the nerve?)	
6	*First sex trauma*	71
	(We just did it—are we ever going to get over it?)	
7	*Are we going out yet?*	79
	(That strange in-between relationship time we all know and love to hate)	
8	*I'm seeing someone*	87
	(Why guys are weird around your friends)	
9	*The call of the wild*	95
	(Getting along with his horrible friends)	
10	*Sex hassles*	101
	(How to avoid the daily bump 'n' grind)	
11	*Hex that ex*	109
	(Why she must be banished for good)	

12 *How to say I love you* — 121
  (Without sounding like Céline Dion)

13 *Meet the parents* — 129
  (And live to moan about it)

14 *Your place, or mine?* — 135
  (Contemplating the dilemmas of life-swapping)

15 *When he thinks your taste is suspect* — 145
  (Or, when smart lovers have silly fights)

16 *You don't bring me flowers* — 151
  (Or, baby, where did our love go?)

17 *Relationship ambiguity, modern girl and guy style* — 159
  (Or, don't you want me, baby?)

18 *Mating calls* — 167
  (That strange phase when he—or even she—flirts with others)

19 *The pointing of the toilet lid* — 175
  (And a thousand other domestic conundrums)

20 *PMS for boys* — 183
  (Or, why the female of the species is deadlier than the male about six days a month)

21 *How to mend a hurting heart* — 193
  (Or, how to have a good break-up)

22 *The Ultimate Chapter* — 201
  When is he supposed to propose?
  (And so on)

A glossary of all things magical and enchanted — 213

Index — 223

Acknowledgments — 231

Introduction

*R*elationships are a bit like deciding where to live—there's a *lot* of stuff to think about. If you move to a small town, you'll have a nice quiet environment, maybe more intimate friendships, and perhaps you'll meet some quirky characters just like the ones in *Ed* or *Northern Exposure*. If you move to the city, you'll have tall buildings, great skim milk cappuccinos to take out, cool vintage clothing shops, and an endless supply of busyness. Where will you be happy?

Like new towns, new relationships are weird places, too. Every guy brings with him a myriad of complexities—he's got moods, clothes, habits, bedrooms, hobbies, parents, a past, ex-girlfriends, and more. There's a lot of stuff to negotiate. And being a magically modern girl, you've already got a life to get on with.

So how can magic and spells make finding a relationship, or being in a relationship, any easier? The thing is, most relationships are not endless tough work but, rather, a series of endlessly puzzling moments that strike an emotional chord. There are a whole lot of questions that come up, with every situation, so for you—wonderful woman that you are—it may seem like it's your duty to ponder the meaning of every single one of those situations. This can be extremely time-consuming and, at the end of the day, you still may not have actually done anything about solving your love dilemma.

That's where magic and spells come in. I am not suggesting you eschew the time-honored tactics of:

- Having coffee with three girlfriends to compare notes on men;
- Empathizing with the characters in *Sex and the City*;
- Going shopping; or
- Cutting your hair.

But this is a world where bad haircuts are plentiful, where girlfriends give you advice based on the phase of their menstrual cycle, where there are only twelve new episodes of your favorite TV show each year, and where credit card debt is out of control. So this book is going to go to the magical source and give you some real inspiration to help you work out your next move.

Instead of staying awake and boiling with rage, while he snores soundly in oblivious boyville, you can cast a spell to help you:

- Feel better;
- Sleep; and
- Figure out the best strategy to change things.

We'll be asking Aphrodite, the goddess of love and beauty, and Diana, the goddess of the hunt and the moon (and an expert on girlfriends), to chime on in, so you will have a whole lot of help to get you through the minefield of love. Just think of this book as your magical secret weapon.

What this book won't do

- It won't change him;
- It won't mean some guy simply gets conjured up;
- It won't make him commit; and
- It won't make a bad guy good.

What this book will do

- Help you meet heaps of guys;
- Sort the absolutely no-ways from the maybe babys;
- Help you let go of the memory of that ex which is crushing your chances at true love;
- Help you understand why your special guy is acting that way (hint: he's a man);
- Help you trick/cajole/manage him into better behavior; and
- Have him acknowledge that you are not only a goddess, but that you are *his* goddess (and help you feel that way, too . . .).

Why you may be man-free right now

Boy, do we live in interesting times. Get this. Hardly anyone's in a traditional couple situation any more. And these days, sex isn't the reason why people get together and stay together. And it's a fact that less and less people are having kids. Fast-forward twenty years time from now, and hardly anyone's going to have a traditional family. That's enough to do anyone's head in.

So now you see what you're up against. I haven't even got started on the modern dilemmas of guys who like guys, and guys who like guys *and* girls. The point is, the world is a-changing. Remember—we are the fallout generation.

Have a little perspective

So, when things on the meeting and mating front get a little tough, take time to put your dilemma into context. There's not so much a drought going on as a complete change in the rituals of our culture—yep, rituals. We don't sashay along to church in our Sunday best with our mom and dad and eight brothers and sisters any more, making eyes at the handsome preacher's son, who responds to the mere batting of our eyelashes by coming around every Sunday for home-made lemonade and, in one year's time, asks our daddy for our hand.

No. These days we see some guy across the other side of a crowded nightclub, have a shouted conversation with him over the blaring music, and try to figure out if we should be swapping love-juice before sun-up. Sounds simple but, oh, what a tangled web we modern girls have to weave our way out of.

So the old-time rituals, meeting places, clothes, manners and gender roles are missing—and that's what we're going to replace here, with some sexy magical work. Only the spells in this book are going to be used to strengthen you and give you determination, support, and power. It's not about throwing your willpower around; it's about having a magical guide to help you work your way through life's maze.

So how do magic and spells work?

Spells work because beneath all the sci-fi, superficial changes that have taken place in the world, people have remained much the same. It doesn't take a lot to throw us out, or to bring us back; so a little magic won't hurt anyone. Casting spells is about getting hooked back into the great cosmic circuitboard, understanding what brings you closer to another soul, and realizing what actions raise good vibes and dismiss bad vibes. And we shouldn't neglect what makes you want him, how love works, how sex works, how men work, and why we still find being together as soul mates the most satisfying trip to take.

It's called love

Every single person out there—no matter how completely deranged or sociopathic—has this awesome, undeniable yearning to be loved, to make meaningful eye contact while naked between clean sheets. It's what we're born for. All of us.

> *And love can make you happy,*
> *And love can make you crazy,*
> *And love can make you scared.*

And not having love can fool you into thinking you're unlovable, or that the world doesn't revolve round those crazy urges to get naked. But everyone is lovable.

No matter how successful you are, how rich you may be, how powerful you get, you still want that quivery feeling. Why? Because it makes us human.

And magic makes us love a whole lot better. So let's get into it.

1
The essentials of spellcasting (How to use magic and spells)

*E*very single modern girl out there could handle a little magic in her messy, busy, modern life. In this crazy, fantastic era, we have become separated from our magical selves, so we hardly ever get down to the beach at full moon and soak up the powerful vibes it pours over the earth (that's a clue—try doing it and you will feel wild).

And our love lives are more than a bit weird. At best, we get along and are madly in love with each other, but we still have those moments where complete incomprehension takes hold. Working daily magic in the form of these spells will help to put you back in touch with the sacred side of life, and enable you to make positive changes—simply, safely, magically—every day that you wish.

Before you start to work magic and cast spells, it is important to set aside a place where you can do your magical work in some kind of privacy. Even if you live in a mad, hippy, "love the one you're with"-type household and it's your turn to share your feelings at the house meeting, do not tell people about your magical spellwork. This is not because anything you are about to discover through practicing magic is in any way evil or scary (all the spells within this book are designed to work for the greater good of all). It's because silence helps to bind a spell. If you keep quiet about it, you can feel the spell's power actually building. If you chat about it, you can feel its potency literally draining away. So one of the magical golden rules is a bit of quiet, please.

The second golden rule is to give it some time. You need to allow magic to work, and impatience, or that frustrated "damn, I gave it five days and I'm still not married to my one and only true love" feeling has to be controlled. Thinking negatively about any project before its time has come, ceasing to give it the nourishment of your faith, will literally stomp the magic out. Any project that you're secretly cynical about will experience a dissipation of energy, so it's going to wilt before it's had time to work. It is wise to adhere to the 95/5 percent rule—95 percent doing, five percent discussing. This is one way to increase positive results in magic, or in any old area of your life you want to kick-start and set in motion.

Here's an analogy. If you plant a little tree, you need to water and care for it and give it the right soil. And when a tiny green shoot pokes up through the earth you've tended, you don't say "Aaargh! That's not a tree, that's a pathetic, tiny little green thing!" and stomp on it in your high heels, do you? I hope you don't, anyway. If you do, you now know why not very much at all is growing in your garden.

Get it? It's pretty much the same with love and magic. Give it time, give it nourishment, give it love—magic, like nature, will absolutely 100 percent work under the right conditions.

How to create a magical space

Every girl needs a magical place to call her own. It doesn't have to be a wacky New Age cathedral or a whole acre of virgin forest complete with free-range unicorn and roaming elf-people. It can just be a corner of your bedroom or study, or a largish area within your house or garden, if you're lucky enough to have the space. If you live with other people, you don't have to go crazy and demand that your roommates shift the TV from the living room because you're making an altar there.

There are many ways you can create this space. Here is one suggestion that works for me and many of my friends.

Find a low table that you like the look of, and place some pictures of someone you find strong and powerful on it. I personally respond well to Joan Jett, Buffy the Vampire Slayer, mermaids, and sea shells. Most magic girls know that found objects are especially significant, and can really rev up your psychic energy. Autumn leaves will remind you of the ever-changing wheel of fortune and fate that we are all ruled by, which allows us to learn the very tricky art of letting go. So will seahorse skeletons, fossils, and anything that is a testament to its past: life moves on. We're all just voyagers on fate's endless sea of change.

Oops, sorry, came over all mystical then . . .

Remember to keep your witchy moments nice and quiet. It's your life, so no-one else needs to know about your magical side. By the way, that includes nosy yet caring parents with whom you still may shelter. And this especially applies if you live with feral neo-sceptics who splutter with laughter when you tell them all about your discovery of the Craft. Just don't go there. Don't seek the approval of people you know are incapable of giving it, and don't ask them to get involved in what is essentially your own business.

When you have chosen your very own special and magical place, you will need to cleanse it thoroughly. Apart from a down-to-earth, practical clean (needless to say, using only earth-friendly cleaning products), you will also need to rework the energy pattern in your chosen space.

You see, wherever you are at any time, there's an energy pattern already in place. It's in the walls, the floor, the ceiling, the leaves, the bark, the sand, and even the concrete. The moment one thing within it changes, it all changes—kind of like a stone thrown into a pond sending out ripples upon ripples. The air within the space carries time. As time goes by the energy shifts, but if the same sorts of things have happened in the same place over and over again, the energy is going to begin to become quite a powerful entity. So you need to get it freshened up, revived and reworked to suit your best purposes and intentions.

Hmm. Amazing, isn't it? This energy cleanse and recharge is a process that can benefit virtually any kind of space (let's not even start on your career—or the trunk of your car). For the moment, let's focus on the sacred space where you will work your magic for love.

Space clearing magical exercise

So, you've chosen your magical corner of the world.

    First, clean it.

The Essentials of Spellcasting

Second, clap your hands together throughout the room or the space. If you can't get a moment to yourself and you feel a bit silly, put some music on so it looks like you're dancing. Just make sure it's the kind of music you want charging your magic and your space. You'll notice when you're clapping that some areas of the space sound dead and muffled, with no resonance. Keep clapping, trying different rhythms and beats till the resonance starts happening—it will, by the way. This means that something has started to shift.

Do this all throughout the space, right up to the top (you don't want a cloud of stale, weird old energy hanging over you) and into all the corners, right down to the floorboards. If you've got carpet, really, really clean it if you intend on keeping it—it's a great hanger-on of stale energy. Energy actually gets bogged down in its fibers, and you can't sweep it away like you can with floorboards. Think about it.

Once you've felt the energy and tone of your claps shift and vibrate differently, burn some of your favorite incense or oil. Sandalwood is a great essential oil for magical clearing and sacred protection, and bergamot is another one that's excellent for keeping you bound to positive, uplifting spirits and etheric manifestations. Don't get spooked—if anything, you're reducing your chances of encountering freaky spirits and gooey etheric plasma creatures by doing this clear-out. (Spirits, by the way, usually feel like loads of weighty energy settling on you. It's not nice, not harmful either, but it can bring you down. If you're not a strong character, or if you're quite young, it tends to happen at around 3.00 a.m., and it can really do your head in. If you do find this is happening, or if there are any other bad feelings oozing around, clap your hands three times and tell the presence firmly but kindly to go away. Then do a space clearing the next day—it'll soon wobble off elsewhere.)

While the oil or incense is burning, get a Tibetan bell and ring it (you can buy one from any esoteric shop). I don't think there's a better magical tool. Tibetan bells are blessed and strong, and are living proof of the power and truth of gentle magic. Ringing the bell will really seal the bad stuff out, and get your head into a beautiful place—strong, wise and funny. Where you feel it sounds best is the right place to ring it. If the room just needs a delicate touch, little tinkly rings will be fine. If there's a strong vibe making you feel like really ringing that bell, then shake it, baby. It's up to you; there's no wrong way—just do what feels right.

Finally, place a white candle on the ground, and sprinkle some sea salt around its base in an anti-clockwise direction. Light it up. Keep a careful watch (for safety reasons—nothing spooky) and, after it has burned down, bury the wax remnants in the garden, or local park if you live in an apartment. (If you're interested in prophecy, by the way, check out the wax remnants before you bury them. What do you see? What comes to mind? Go with your instant impulse—don't try to analyze or question it. Then bury the wax. Weird things can come up. One of mine was once a pizza. Guess what my first meal with a future boyfriend was?)

Every person working with spell magic is advised to create this sacred space. Caring for it on a regular basis is a simple yet profound ritual in itself—one that will restore healing energy and help focus your mind, body, and spirit on magical matters. Its beautiful appearance will be an enduring symbol of the love you have for your magical work and for yourself.

Any time you feel the energy in your home or magical space getting stuck, just perform this ritual and you'll clear the air—literally. The good news is that keeping this space positive and beautiful will also bring a new dimension of peace to your house, and a sacred symbol to your home.

You can tend and groom your own special magical space each and every day, if you like. Or just when you feel like it's necessary.

You can place fresh fruit upon your altar (an orange makes a natural incense holder—just poke the sticks in) and spend a few quiet moments there at the beginning of each day. I hate to say it, but the earlier the better—sunrise is a very magical time of day.

Care for it by cleaning and rearranging your symbols and stones. You now have a peaceful and calming little ritual to enjoy every day.

Being an enchantress

Spells that are motivated by positive intentions encourage true change, growth, and self-development in a girl's life. Spells that are motivated by greed, envy, anger, resentment, and petty negativity will erode your magical abilities and hurt your heart.

Here are some golden rules for magical spellcasters.

Take responsibility for what you are wishing for

With the law of three by three humming inside your mind, remember that what you wish for, in every respect, you will get back to the power of three. Now, rather than this meaning you are incredibly powerful and everything will be perfect, it actually means that yes, you are incredibly powerful, so please, be responsible when casting spells. Nobody expects you to be a boring perfect magic girl. You are going to have all the usual emotionally suspect moments that everyone has. You are, I know, not going to come over all perfectly Zen and spiritual and experience total calm and control forever. Besides, how bland would life be? But when you spellcast, when you're in the moment, if you direct energy at an individual who you know in your heart isn't the right one for you, if you play with people for all the wrong reasons, it will only bring you pain in the long run—it's called karma.

So be certain that you cast for you, and mostly for good results. If you do take responsibility, you'll have thought your feelings through and come to some kind of arrangement with yourself—a spiritual deal, if you like. You have to hand it over to the Universe, or surrender, as many New Age types say. Despite the cringey vocabulary, they're right. Be responsible, use freedom of choice, do the work, then give it up. One more time for those of you up in back who didn't quite catch what I said. You cast the spell, you work on yourself, and let the Universe do the work. Learn to trust the way it works—it'll be good for the rest of your life, too, not just for finding true love.

Center your energy when spellcasting

If your emotional state is out of whack, if you are stressed out and upset, your spellwork could well end up all over the place, too. Always calm yourself by chanting affirmations, candle-gazing, or by doing whatever makes you feel relaxed and calm. Then you can work some real magic.

If you are enraged, you absolutely have to wait until the intensity of your feelings has passed—so no crazed jealousy or rebound spells, please.

Scrub up your psyche

Bathe by blue or white candlelight to help wash away negative or stale energy in your auric field. Breathing in color also helps. Take in some nice, slow deep breaths of calming, beautiful or energizing colors while lying in a safe place—your bed, the herb garden, the beach—until you feel clear and ready for action. Try breathing in blues for calm, or white for all-round cosmic and psychic cleansing and purification.

Nurture yourself

And I mean all the time. Working spells is all about making positive changes, and transformation. Okay, and meeting men with whom you can develop your very own true love story.

However, as everything on this planet is connected, to achieve anything good at all and certainly anything magical, you must truly love and care for yourself first. That means you eat well, and you don't abuse your body with too much junk food. I know eating unhealthy food is absolutely necessary from time to time, but truly, if you do want to work magic, at least make an attempt to eat well. You'll be amazed at the difference it makes to your headspace. Even if it seems extreme, eat organic foods if possible and do your best to eat food that you know is nourishing, fresh, in season, and natural. Why? Fast foods are full of poison, and poison lowers the energy of your auric field. It's as simple as that.

The same goes for alcohol—it's a depressant, and while a tiny bit of a drink like a fine red wine is okay (if you're legal), the problem is that too much alcohol can seriously disrupt your psychic powers. It also depresses your entire physiological system, and inclines you to hangovers, moodiness, bad skin, and one-night stands with entirely inappropriate candidates for your heart's attention—not to mention toxic build-up in both your physical and etheric bodies. Your body will look and feel bad, and you'll suffer mood swings as well as waking up with all the wrong people.

Now, I admit to being biased. These days I don't drink, because I never used to stop drinking when I did. The thing is that I wasn't alone. Drinking cocktails can be gorgeous and glamorous—one cocktail, with girlfriends. But trying to keep up when drinking with the boys—forget it. And it was amazing how much my life, magic, career and love life improved when I quit drinking forever.

So I guess you can imagine that I'm going to have a little talk with you now about drugs. If you've any interest whatsoever in magic, please don't listen or give any credence to those people who think that psychotropic drugs take you closer to some kind of true cosmic experience. They don't. They just don't. I've read *New Scientist* on this, and psychotropics are super-dangerous for loads of reasons. They can lead to crashing cars, ending up with psychosis, walking happily into traffic and so on. But one majorly scary thing that not too many people know is that psychotropics actually lower a chemical in your brain called serotonin. Those of you who know your brain chemistry will already know that lower serotonin levels in your brain make you feel really low. Lower than low. Sometimes suicidal. If the levels stay low, or get interfered with and can no longer regulate themselves, you could be in for long-term bouts of serious depression.

So please don't mess with your brain. It's a whole lot more complicated than what people say—it's not about killing brain cells (which drugs and alcohol do), it's also about killing or disrupting the brain's very own system of checks and balances. It's like pouring toxic chemicals into water and drinking it, for fun. Don't pollute your mind—it truly is one of the earth's most delicate ecosystems. Don't mess with your brain—it's who you are.

Sleep well

Get plenty of sleep—you'll feel great and you'll look amazing. (Did you know that sleep is now being cited as the latest Hollywood trend? The rich and famous are heading out to luxury palaces to snooze in for 10 to 12 hours.) A good night's sleep will make you look and feel fantastic. So sleep. It's a beautiful and beautifying thing. Sleep also means dreams, and these are the true friends of witches and spell casters.

Exercise sensibly and on a regular basis

Just stretching every day will make your spells work better. A 40-minute walk or run in the morning will level your moods, kick-start your metabolism, and make you a vivid, healthy, and ambient soul. It'll amp up your life force, the strength of which is exactly the thing that makes you attractive.

Trust in your inner self

You are your own best adviser. Try meditation techniques for really getting in touch with your intuition, which will help when life is getting gnarly.

Try not to be reactive. If you are finding that you have to trust your wits, practice making sharp decisions in a low-key environment first, to take the pressure off you when you actually do have the pressure on. (If you know what I mean. Of course you do. It's all about practice, isn't it?)

Create more and more love in your life

Energy makes energy, love makes love, and hate hurts your heart. First of all, love thyself. To thine own self be true—all of that. Making love work in your life starts with acknowledging that by beating yourself up, you're just adding to the pain in the world. Be a being of light. Don't be a destroyer.

Breathe fresh air

Please, please, please give up smoking. Breathing fresh oxygen is one of the human body's greatest needs to function well. The vibrations of clean air are naturally higher than those of polluted air. Not to mention the tragic fact that smoking makes your breath smell like Satan's bottom, turns your skin yellow and creates dry and wrinkled skin around your mouth. They're not the gorgeous, "I love my life" lines that we all should adore—they're the tragic, "I smoked a pack a day and only just realized it made me smell and look haggard" kind of lines.

Smoking kills you. And if you're dead, you can't find love. Not on this plane, anyway.

The rules of spellcasting

Before casting your spell, visualize a circle of white light around your sacred space. Then, say a little prayer to the goddess, or whatever you want. Praying for Universal kindness and good will do, or to the Dalai Lama is equally as cool, so is Chrissie Hynde or Madonna. Just focus and spread a little joy and peace around before you do your work.

There are two magic methods that really, really work, two simple ways to work with the spells here in *Love Magic*. And, okay, they're not really all that simple. But you can chop and change, so don't panic. Be intuitive with your approach, and scientific in your method. Huh? Well, let me explain a little bit.

First of all, allow the Universe to help you choose which spell will be the most beneficial to you. Take this book and, with your eyes closed, flick casually through its pages, allowing yourself to breathe softly. As the life issue you most wish to receive magical guidance on solidifies in your mind's eye, stop flicking. This is the magical work the Universe declares will most help you in the present moment.

The second way is simply to choose which spell you wish to work on. If you decide to work your magic this way, be aware that you need to make your choice with the knowledge that with choice comes responsibility. Be sure to work your spell with the very best and highest of intentions.

How to store and reenergize your spells

Store your book in your sacred place—your dressing table, or by the bed, or someplace where you feel really safe and girly. If the book's energy feels a little "worn" to you, simply wrap it in black silk for protection, and place a quartz crystal on top of it for several days to recharge it.

However, if you flick to the same spell again and again, the Universe is gently pointing out to you that there is an issue that needs healing in your life.

If a page randomly falls open, or for some reason seems to "leap out" at you, pay attention. This is no accident, and you would be clever to consider working that spell as, again, the Universe is trying to get your attention.

Magical pointers

There are many elements involved in creating a powerful and successful spell. Consult the lists below before casting your spells to make them as potent and magical as possible.

Magical days of the week

Sunday: the most auspicious day for spells involving ambition, pride, issues of power and control, success, and anything that involves literally "shining" at an activity, legal success, breakthroughs, births, praise, or little children.

Monday: a great day for psychic development, intuition, dreams, the domestic sphere, visions, hunches, detective work, and soul mates.

Tuesday: try casting spells for courage, action, sexuality, conflict, confrontation, travel, progress, determination, self-protection, training, and physical workouts on this day.

Wednesday: spells relating to discussion, verbal agreements, learning, quick-thinking processes, impulsive action, drama, the written word, and gossip should be cast on Wednesday.

Thursday: a good spell day for legal matters, political motivation, wealth, business matters, strategy, takeovers, insurance, and hard, clear, practical thinking.

Friday: is the day for casting spells of compassion, romance, lovers, beauty, melody, song, the natural world, the earth, flowers, birds, any artistic endeavor, creativity, love letters, and sensuality.

Saturday: this chillout day is the best time to cast spells for karmic law, material gain, property, merchandising, wills, borrowing, lending, outcomes from business ventures, ending relationships and closure of matters of the heart.

Magical properties of herbs

Love: apple, basil, dill, jasmine, frangipani, honeysuckle, and rose.

Prosperity: allspice, cedar, comfrey, ginger, yam, and kumara.

Protection: bay, clove, fennel, pine, and witch hazel.

Health: nutmeg, oak, and rue.

Fertility: fig, geranium, mustard, patchouli, and poppy.

Happiness: catnip, celandine, hawthorn, marjoram, and lavender.

Courage: poke, yarrow, lime, cedarwood, frankincense, and rosewood.

Magical meanings of colors

White: purifies, cleanses, and energizes on a spiritual level.

Pink: represents love, friendship, self-love, confidence, family love, brotherly and sisterly love, and gatherings of all kinds of peers.

Red: strengthens the passionate side of your nature, raises sexual energy, and intensifies emotional levels.

Orange: allows the power of attraction to be increased and is a positive color with radiant energy. It is very good for people who wish to increase their physical energy, but it is too strong for people who are weak or unwell.

Yellow: increases concentration and focus, and allows mental breakthroughs to occur. Too much can lead to obsessiveness, so use sparingly or infrequently.

Green: promotes growth, freshness, health, new stars, abundance, and the healing energy of nature.

Turquoise: brings happiness, light spirit, clear thinking, and good cheer. This color helps with mental balance, the inner self, and psychic ability.

Blue: is a healing color, used for spells involving protection, water, strength, and clarity.

Purple: is a majestical color that helps with victory, serious intent, loyalty, and affiliation.

Violet: enhances the perception of dreams, spiritual matters, higher self, and peaceful intentions.

Gold: not surprisingly represents wealth and confidence. This color can also be used for strength of purpose and inner belief in a positive outcome.

Brown: represents wisdom, the earth, natural healing, intuitive knowledge, ancient power, stable nature, and force for balance.

Moon magic

The moon has been the magical focus of witches and mystics for thousands of years. Its silvery light can inspire healing, wisdom, hope and happiness—as well as stimulate true psychic power. Listed here are the phases of the moon and their magical meanings.

The new moon
This is a wonderful time for new beginnings and growth. When you wish to cast a spell to favor a symbolic birth or a new start in your life—whether it is love, money, a new relationship, job, or friendship—the new moon is the time to do it. Or, if you wish to renew or recharge the energy in an aspect of your life, then this is the most auspicious phase of the moon for you.

The waxing moon
The waxing moon is the period of time from the new moon to the next full moon. This is the phase during which the moon's symbolic and magical power strengthens with each passing second. Use its magic to promote empowering spells that are designed to promote steady growth in an aspect of your life.

The waning moon
The waning moon is the period from the peak of the full moon to the next new moon. During this time, the moon's power is symbolically draining away, making this a time for spells that banish heartache, or end sadness or negative influences in your life. It is a time for letting go.

The full moon
The full moon is the most powerful and magical phase of the moon. It is the perfect time to cast spells, work charms, and generally revel in the increased energy and psychic power this phase brings. Use the enchanted power of the full moon to see the fruits of your magical labors become reality.

The magical law of three times three

The law of the threefold return is perhaps the most important ethic of working magic. The number three is very powerful; it symbolizes the sending out, the manifestation, and then the returning karmic influence—three important steps of spellcasting. Whatever you send out in spellwork will come back to you to the power of three.

This is a natural law, and it's a wonderful incentive to keep your intentions as high as possible. By obeying the law of the threefold return, you will be creating positive experiences for yourself and for others.

Please be assured that positive magic brings about the most powerful results of all. When you wish for fulfilling, loving experiences and are mindful of your thoughts and actions, always seeking to go for the highest possible choice, for the greatest good of all, you will reap far more benefits than if you are thinking in old, musty, faded patterns.

What every witchy girl needs

Here's a list of all the things that a modern witchy woman needs in this lifetime. No tie-dye, no mung beans and no long, unconditioned, center-parted hair required . . .

- Book of Shadows;
- A good tarot deck;
- Some essential oils;
- A herb garden (or just herbs);
- A witchy calendar;
- A sacred little place;
- Some colored cloth;
- Some colored thread and ribbons;
- Candles; and
- Natural, found objects, like shells, flowers, and stones.

Add plenty of positive energy, good health, and self-esteem and you're on your way to becoming a bona fide witchy woman.

Book of Shadows

A Book of Shadows is a work of magic in itself. It is a sacred tool that will help you realize your magical workings, and will evoke the power of magic in your everyday life—and in your relationships, your work and your friendships. Magic is about change, so your Book of Shadows is where you can reflect, safely and magically, on what particular magic is working for you.

Many witches decorate their Book of Shadows symbolically, so go for it. (Think of the sisters in *Charmed*—their Book of Shadows is divine.) Tailor your Book of Shadows to echo who you are and who you want to be—record all your hopes and dreams. Nothing is too silly or pretentious within its pages.

Traditionally, all witches and covens kept a Book of Shadows. But you should never see another witch's individual copy—it's respected and very private. I wouldn't want to read anyone's Book of Shadows because it's massively bad karma. Be very private about yours—you don't need to let anyone know it even exists. The minute you involve others, its subtle magic can change. So keep it your special secret and your Book of Shadows will become your proven and trusted magical guide.

Essential list of essential oils

Eucalyptus

Uses: bath, inhalation, massage into head, forehead, and chest.

What it does: eucalyptus cleanses, soothes, and purifies. It can clear your head and help you to think rationally. It will make you powerful, as you will be able to rise above impulse and think clearly, calmly and less emotionally.

Rose geranium

Uses: bath, massage, oil burner.

What it does: geranium is a hormone balancer, so it's great for when you feel your moods are going to get you into some serious trouble. It won't leave you like a zombie, but will boost your energy and keep you in control of your emotions.

Bergamot

Uses: massage, oil burner, cleaning, drinking—as in Earl Grey tea.

What it does: bergamot is a beautiful, uplifting, joyful fragrance, and is great for protection. It is also a restorative, so use it after a long night of . . . whatever it was you two got up to that has left you so drained. The aroma actually makes you smell likeable, so it's for winning people over.

Rosemary

Uses: a tiny bit in the bath, as a rinse for bella curly hair, also great for a scalp massage.

What it does: rosemary restores concentration and it also stimulates your memory, so it's great for exams or to remember the name of the cute guy you met last night.

Chamomile

Uses: bath, body, hair rinse for blondes.

What it does: chamomile is a real downer, in the best possible way. It soothes you, leaving you feeling all serene and gracious—so use it when the stress of having too many dates is starting to take its toll! However, it's also extremely sensual, so you'll be calm, sexy and languid. Hmm . . .

Neroli

Uses: bath, inhalation, burner, and spells.

What it does: neroli is a great loosener, so use it if you want to get into a chatty party mode. This magical, uplifting oil actually gets men really relaxed too—but not so relaxed that they cannot pleasure you. Ahem.

Ylang Ylang

Uses: massage, oil burner, inhalation, and bathing.

What it does: this precious oil goes straight to work on frizzy emotions, by smoothing them down and relaxing any tangled thoughts. It's the perfect soothing blend after a stressifying day, leaving you chilled out and ready to embrace the best of your boy.

Lavender

Uses: cleaning, massage, inhalation, bathing, and purifying.

What it does: lavender is the oil every witchy girl ought to have. It relieves stress, tackles insomnia, makes you feel radiantly calm and is an antiseptic, so it's a powerful beauty treatment and skin healer. Great for toning down the volume of your anger, it throws cool water on nerves of fire and sorts out those jangled thoughts of jealousy. Pour drops into a bath, and watch your all-over blush of anger fade into alabaster beauty.

Rose

Uses: massage, inhalation, oil burner, and spells.

What it does: rose is the very essence of true and romantic love. This rare and precious oil makes you smile and enhances any hint of sensuality, making you feel va va va bloom, smell scrumptious and look like an angel who's lost her wings.

Frankincense

Uses: cleansing sacred space, oil burner, and spellwork.

What it does: this sacred oil is a strong aphrodisiac with a tendency to make you want to try some new techniques—maybe a strange erotic scenario, share your fantasies, lick luscious substances from each other's hips—so be ready for the experimental side of your sensual nature. Go the distance, and greet the dawn with a sex kitten purr, a deliciously tired body and a cream-licking smile on your pretty face.

Myrrh

Uses: massage, spellwork, and increasing psychic powers.

What it does: myrrh consists of chemical compounds that are remarkably similar to the smell of a freshly washed love god—thus this is one of the great revitalizing love potions. It's superb for those saucy times when you're all alone, but are feeling a little restless. Just burn six drops in your burner and close your eyes, and as the first tendril of perfume captures your imagination your very own dream lover will be conjured up.

Sandalwood

Uses: protective powers, moisturizing, inhalation, massage, and diffusion.

What it does: if your love vibes are a little out of cosmic whack, or if someone's upset you and you're feeling a little on the delicate side, burn this clarifying and protective sacred oil. Its speciality is dissipating nasty vibes. You'll soon be sighing contentedly, wondering what there ever was to fret about. If someone's been just a wee bit too clingy, or even possessive, this will buy you some much cherished time out for as long as you need.

Clary sage

Uses: massage, oil burner, bathing, and diffusion.

What it does: hmm, scent of a he-man. A prince of oils, this lush, silky aromatic contains delicious-smelling, masculine-type plant hormones that make you think of seasons spent making love in a hammock under the hot sun—and never getting burned. It's uplifting, too. Make sure you dilute it with a base oil before applying it to your skin, as it's rather powerful. Then lie back and enjoy its divine, regal ambience.

Jasmine

Uses: massage, inhalation, bathing and diffusion.

What it does: jasmine has a little secret—indole. Indole smells faintly of newly washed and scented flesh, so it's simultaneously the most indulgent and anti-depressing of aphrodisiacs. A boon for the newly smitten to bathe in.

Your very own magical cards

The origins of the tarot deck are too old to remember. The main thing to know is that their ancient and unique spiritual imagery has been used for centuries as a tool for insight and prophecy for witchy types. I believe that the tarot is still the best tool around for relevant, easy to understand and practical magical guidance.

There are many wonderful decks available. Quality versions include instructions and spreads—but, as it is all about intuition, simply handling the cards and experimenting with them yourself is the best approach.

How to be a witchy woman in four easy steps

1. Develop your intuition

Okay, so you want to know what people are really thinking, whether he's the one or just another Mr. Maybe, or whether that new guy at work is really interested. Here are some simple ways to develop your intuition—and more importantly, how to trust it.

Set aside a few minutes at the beginning and the end of each day to do this exercise. Start by sitting comfortably in a quiet place, and start to breathe deeply. Unlike meditation, though, we're going to take a look at what may be happening for you today. Don't try to force any thoughts into your mind—there is a big difference between paranoia and intuition, and between imagination and intuition. Knowing these differences is what will make you far more psychic in the long run—and able to act on those intuitive messages.

Take a few minutes to think about the person or situation you wish to know more about and watch for these physical symptoms:

- Hairs standing up on the back of your neck;
- Nervousness;
- Your heart beating faster;
- Breath coming in shorter;
- Temperature rise; and
- Doubt or apprehension.

If you have a persistent thought—one that comes back time and again—pay attention to it. More than likely it's nagging you for a good reason.

2. *Fine-tune your dream reading*

Ditto for dreams that go on and on with the same themes.

I have a recurring dream that takes place in a building—sometimes it's a house. Other times an apartment or warehouse. Not every element of the dream is the same. I have looked for hidden jewels in one version. Often, the building is somewhere I feel I've lived. Sometimes there have actually been frightening people or symbols in this dream, or an entire section of the building might give way. However, all of these dreams have the same kinds of things in common—in particular floorboards that were none too firm underfoot, making it difficult for me to see the fantastic water view out the windows. The dreams always felt like I was somewhere that could be fabulous—I just had to do a lot of work to realize the potential of the place.

No prizes for guessing this dream's symbology. The run-down and unpredictable dream house was about two important issues in my own life—stability and enrichment. You see, the house in my dream symbolized me. The clues to what I needed to work on in my life are the rickety floorboards, hidden jewels and the fantastic view. If the dream house is made safe and stable, the jewels will be found, and the view enjoyed. Repairing myself would mean creating a safe, stable and nurturing environment. Under those conditions, I could reach my potential—and like what I see.

You should begin to keep your own version of a dream dictionary. What means one thing to me will mean nothing to you, so it's best to diarize it all. Use your Book of Shadows if you like, just to keep all nice, witchy things together.

Your intuition really is at its savviest when you combine cool thinking with gut instinct—it's a winning combination. Move those desires and love feelings aside when assessing how you think a situation may move forward. People are who they are—and they aren't going to change just because you lavish them with affection and pour out your emotions. Here are some major pointers to getting in touch with what your smartest self is saying to you:

- Acknowledge your feelings. You don't have to find reasons or justify why you feel a certain way, either. Just notice and respect how you feel about something. This doesn't mean react, such as quitting your job, or relationship, just because you suddenly feel like it. It means just honor whatever it is you're feeling at the time.
- Notice what your body does when you're with the person or in a situation you want to know more about.
- If you are stalling or hesitating regarding a commitment to dates or lifetimes together, notice that too. Are you a commitment-phobe, or is there something you're avoiding?

Preparing to remember

Dreams can lead you to hot men—yes, they really can—but you've got to remember some shifty little things. If you want to get into a week of insightful dreaming, go to bed at the same time each night. Try lighting some evocative incense in your bedroom, and drink a cup of soothing chamomile tea before you go to bed. Be sure to keep your Book of Shadows close by, so you can record your dreams when you wake up.

As you feel yourself drifting off, chant this invocation three times:

> *Sights for my mind,*
> *Knowledge for my heart,*
> *Strange treasures unwind,*
> *Let the dreaming start.*

Pay particular attention to any of the following images in your dreams, and record them:
- Colors;
- Numbers;
- Landscapes;
- Temperatures;
- Physical sensations;
- Where you were;
- Who you were with;
- Were you identifiable as yourself; and
- What feelings did your dream leave you with?

Tell the truth in your Book of Shadows—don't invent, simply seek to understand what was there. Dream symbols have a meaning that's all your very own. Two people dream of a spider: to one person it's good luck; to the other, it denotes fear and danger. Blanket negative definitions tend to be cultural or even generational.

After a week, go through your Book of Shadows and see if there are any patterns emerging in your dreams. Look for crossovers between your waking and dreaming life. Don't believe that everything is as separate as you've been taught it is.

3. Spread a little magical love and kindness every day

You need to send some loving, positive energy every single day. It can be to a loved one, to something you believe in, or just a thank you to the Universe for creating such a beautiful day. A prayer can be putting a frangipani in a china teacup where you'll see its beauty and smell its perfume all day long, playing or listening to beautiful music, singing a song or looking after your frazzled friend's baby for two hours to give her a break. A prayer is anything positive that is done consciously for the good of all.

You leave the world a better place every single day when you go off to sleep and head into dreamland. Do one kind thing every day, and you'll have more good luck and magic than you could believe. It's true—what goes around, comes around.

So write a thank you note, tell someone you love them, be kind to a person who needs a caring hand, and notice the beauty in the everyday. Be gentle for half-an-hour each day. Take a walk in the sunshine and look at the tree tops. Find Venus at night and send a wish to her. Dance without inhibition. Wear amazing colors. Don't hold back on the jasmine oil or red lipstick. Keep your skin pale, as sunburn is not spiritual. Always be aware of the moon and send a wish to her when you need to, or for another, or just to say you love moonlight.

You'll be happier, and the world will be uplifted if you perform these little acts of magical kindness every day.

4. Have you got magic in your soul?

Answer the questions below to find out if you are a witchy woman.

- Have any relatives, near or far, had red hair?
- Do you remember if any female family member ever made their own beauty potions?
- Have you or any relative had the talent of reading the future?
- Has anyone in your family been simply irresistible to the opposite sex?

- Have you ever made an important, life-changing decision based purely on intuition?
- Do people often come to you for love, help or advice?
- Are your dreams prophetic?
- Have you ever felt transported by your dreams to another realm?
- Do animals, especially cats, just love being around you?
- Do you believe that nature is sacred?
- Are you attracted to talismans and symbols?
- Can you feel what someone is about to say or do, before it has actually happened?

If you've answered yes to a skimpy three or more of these questions, you are most definitely going to enjoy and benefit from learning more about magic, because you're a witch at heart already!

When to cast spells during the year

Some people get all worked up over when to do what with spellcasting. Your best guides are your intuition and the phases of the moon, which have already been covered in this book.

If you want your spell to have a little more power, try synchronizing your magic with the following significant times of the year.

Special juju-favorable days of the year

To some people, the whole idea of spellcasting is to be in tune with the seasons and the natural energies of their environment.

Because of this, the traditional times for spells differ in the northern and southern hemispheres. Don't become worried; simply decide what feels best for your purpose, and cast when you decide it is best.

Imbolg, or Candlemas

Imbolg celebrates the beginning of spring—it's actually a true feast of light. The best thing to do during this time is to remember renewal, relish all new beginnings and light candles of yellow, green or white to celebrate the notion of fresh starts for life and love.

When to cast your spells: The day you feel the first hint of spring in the air, when you catch your first whiff of jasmine or wear short sleeves for the first time.

The Equinox

The triumph of light over dark. This is an auspicious time for casting new beginning-type spells.

When to cast your spells: The day you notice it's light far longer than it used to be. The first day you walk home after work in the sun, or you see the sun set after your work day has finished. You will feel the lengthened day better than any calendar can tell you.

Beltane

This is a very sexy celebration. Basically, you get to have hot sex in honor of the fermenting energy of summer. If you don't want to conceive take the necessary precautions, as the sensual and receptive energy of this time can increase your fertility.

When to cast your spells: Start your spellcasting when your sexual appetite increases, and you feel the urge to get sexy outside in the warmth of the night.

Samhain

A mystical time when the spirit guides can help you out—great for connecting with beloved relatives or friends who've passed on. It's also a terrific time to reflect on the year so far.

When to cast your spells: Whenever you feel the carefree days of summer are leaving, then it's time to think back on the days past, the people you've loved, those you may have lost and the lessons you can learn. Also watch out for the first of the deep red leaves—a sure-fire natural signal. Another giveaway is feeling a little haunted by the past, in dreams or thoughts.

Stars and the moon

A little dab of astrology can give a spell some extra bliss.

Moon in Aries: fabulous frissons for start-ups, promotions, love affairs and new titles, like Mrs.?

Moon in Taurus: long, lanky lovers adore Taurean energy. A fab time to bake irresistible love cakes, buy love tokens or even exchange rings.

Moon in Gemini: sexual acts of imagination fare well under this light—extra sexy rapport with your beloved is also recommended under the twin-influenced moon.

Moon in Cancer: romantic love, gifts for the home and nurturing your relationship are all favored during this moon.

Moon in Leo: dramatic spells will gain power at this time, as will spells devoted to beauty, performance and glamor.

Moon in Virgo: detailed spells are best performed now. A favored time to discuss matters of money, your future, or where you'll live.

Moon in Libra: self-awareness spells and rituals for harmony will thrive under this influence.

Moon in Scorpio: psychic protection and enhancement spells will flourish now.

Moon in Sagittarius: an imaginative and good-humored time, this moon phase will benefit anyone wishing to cast spells for friendship and get-togethers.

Moon in Capricorn: a blessed time for spells or work requiring a little more discipline than you're usually keen to bring to a magical project.

Moon in Aquarius: an individualistic sign, this nevertheless is the best time to cast spells for benefiting the good of all involved.

Moon in Pisces: a time to ponder your relationship and cast for more knowledge concerning its qualities.

2

Why isn't he here yet?
(The lament of the single girl)

*L*et us commence by reassuring modern girls of the many social reasons relationships got so damn hard this century. Let us also state now, extremely loudly, that yes, you can overcome the growing epidemic of singledom.

BUT . . . You know how some girls just seem to stay single for ages? And how people look for reasons, mainly to comfort them? There are good reasons for being single through choice, and then there are those other reasons girls stay single—though they proclaim loudly they want to meet a man, life's so unfair, all men suck, and every guy is gay.

Excuse me, but the only reason single girls stay that way is because they actually are either very very fussy (which you have every right to be) or there's something going on—and maybe it's with you. Maybe, just maybe you're single because you are incredibly difficult to have a relationship with, or it could even be something you're totally unaware of, like a vibe you're sending out (Yes, it's scary, isn't it?).

Because, despite the cliché about there being no straight guys, the truth is that there are always guys looking for women to love them—and for them to love, too. There are men who will give you foot rubs, and there are even men who remain fantastic after two dates.

Rule number one: There are loads of guys out there for you to meet and hook up with on a modern kind of permanent basis.

Rule number two: If you haven't met him yet, the Universe and all the goddesses of the past and present are about to give you some spells to get over the big fat roadblocks in the way of your romance.

Some of these roadblocks might include scenarios like:

- You never leave the house;
- You send scary vibes out (come near me and I'll break your heart/drive you insane/criticize your mother);
- You think men suck;
- You think you should have George Clooney, and no-one else will do;

Why Isn't He Here Yet?

- You go out with certified unavailable-type drug addict loser guys who you know will never commit. (Now that's called a block);
- You move around a lot (from town to town, not shimmy-when-you-walk-type movement); and
- You're totally absorbed with someone or something else (which is okay—it's just that you have to make room to make love . . .).

There are a whole lot of other reasons for why you might find yourself suddenly or even chronically single. But even in big cities where gaydom abounds, I have quizzed plenty of females and it's all about attitude.

There are always going to be extenuating circumstances. These can include the fact that you went to an all-girls' school and made not a friend there. You might even have a health condition that makes you feel compelled to run away whenever you see a guy.

But it's more likely to be because of things like:

- You are not prepared risk your heart;
- You are only prepared to risk your heart if he marries you first;
- You make the same mistake endlessly;
- You go with guys just like your ex-boyfriend;
- You're saving yourself for someone who is completely unattainable (chances are you're never going to meet Brad Pitt and even if you do, he's married);
- You think guys who really like you and who treat you right must be losers; and
- You think you have a few flaws to iron out first (but doesn't everyone?).

I know that's heavy to start with. You're probably on the verge of wanting a refund—"this book is mean!" But the heavy stuff, okay the truth, is good—and it's on your side in the hunt for love. Because you're more in control than you thought, so there exists the distinct and exciting possibility of change. And finding love.

The getting wise spell

What is the point of being a smart, modern woman if you haven't figured out guys, how people are and how life is? Getting clued in is imperative for you to see the ramifications of everything you do, every choice you make. You won't obtain the powers of the Delphic Oracle, but you will see how cause and effect works. This seems to be (magically speaking) mostly about perspective—being able to see the long- and short-term karmic impact of action or inaction in a particular, usually challenging situation.

Look upon this as an opportunity to work some magic on your own ability to "see" wisely. If you have a greater inner understanding of the karmic ripples of your decisions, your love life will change for the better.

You may be searching for insight into a particular situation, or maybe you would like to be wiser, altogether, in your life. If so, you are already aware that you may have more to ponder than meets the eye in this situation. Use this spell to help you act in the best interests of your own inner, magical, instinctual self. You are canny—you simply need to be able to channel your intuition consciously, and this magical spell will help you do that every day of your life.

On a Wednesday night, under a waxing moon,
Gather sage, frankincense, rosemary and a handful
of beautiful autumn leaves.
Take a piece of handmade parchment paper,
and a blue pen,
And write the story of your love life.
Write the outcome of your learning.
This pattern you are tracing in ink,
Is your teacher,
Your true wisdom.

*Live your lesson mindfully,
and learn its significance.
After casting this spell, put aside your love lesson
parchment somewhere safe. Have a look at it in six months'
time—have you been living its lessons?*

Love detox

Release from the past. While we all desire it, the problem is that we don't want to lose our past because then we lose a part of who we are. It's akin to whether you keep photos of old boyfriends on view, where they may make you feel sad and drag your energy levels right down. The choice is really up to you. A friend of mine once gave me great advice—I was going to toss every single photo I had of all my old loves, but she gently and sensibly reminded me that I wasn't just throwing them away, I was throwing away my life, too.

So what should you do? Get rid of any image that makes you feel sad, unloved, or teary. Anything that makes you feel better, keep. It's about releasing the negative emotions of the past, but keeping the memories that are worthwhile. It doesn't mean viewing the past with rose-colored glasses, either—it means learning from it and moving on.

At-a-glance magic for single girls

Affirmation: "It is safe to let love into my life."

Day of the week: Friday.

Color: Pink.

Stone: Rose quartz.

Drink: The Cosmopolitan (it's pink!).

Goddesses: Marilyn Monroe (Bus Stop), Madonna (all that ambition), Minerva (too smart for many gods) and Olivia Newton-John (just so sweet!).

Essential oils: Grapefruit, rosewood and patchouli.

Herb: Marjoram—to calm your nerves and slow your biological clock.

3

A few good men: Location, location, location
(Or, where men materialize these days)

*T*his chapter is all about meeting lots of men, working a spell to choose the right one, and working some very important spells to release any crazy longings that may still linger for Mr. Very Wrong. *Heeere* we go, huntress girl.

So, you're doing your homework and making magical space for a guy, but ahh, the practical stuff needs to get done too. Ultimately you need to leave the house (even if you have met him on the net!). But where will you meet him? Here's my all-time hottest witchy tip to meeting men, one recommended by all smart, happy and loved-up women I know—your friends. Most women marry brothers or cousins of friends, friends of friends, or guys they meet through work friends. The deal is that you get to check them out. Most women—and I mean it—do not meet long-term potential spouses at nightclubs, bars, dance parties or by bumping into them while carrying over-stuffed bags of shopping.

It's friends that count. So, let's look at your friends. You do have some, don't you? Okay, for each of these friends, how do they improve your chances of meeting a man? Every female or male friend you have must know some guys. It's just logic. And the thing is, this is where you have to examine the purpose of your friendship.

I'll clarify this. Some people think they're not worth much as friends unless they fulfil some major function or cork some hole in that friend's life. Like, for example, you could be the designated driver 99 percent of the time in your social life. Or you could be perpetually cast in the role of the listener—the friend who holds hands, comforts, feeds, phones, talks through suicidal urges or is the experiment for a pal.

But what do they do for you? Now, if you're sitting there saying we laugh together, we hang out, we meet people, we do social stuff, we get each other through man traumas, she holds my hand when I'm way, way down inside—great. BUT, if you're saying I listen, I feel good when they bring me their problems, I drive them when they're drunk or, even worse, I make them look a whole lot funnier or sexier, you've got a friendship hole. And where there are friendship holes, there are love gaps.

So, let's have a little bit of a magical look at the issues. Oh dear. The magical truth is, it's all about self-esteem—again.

Now, despite appearances, everyone has self-esteem hassles. At the core of every person is a little niggly hole that gets filled with yucky emotional bad-vibe type stuff, and that makes us feel very, very bad indeed. Just so we're clear on this, the feel-bad stuff can come in the form of words or nasty little untruths you tell yourself, like:

- I am fat;
- I am boring;
- I am too old;
- I am too young;
- I am not very interesting;
- I have no money; and
- I am not Jennifer Lopez (my own personal favorite).

That's right, you're not perfect. That's because you're much better than that—you're a real live person. And the great thing about this is that you're interesting, and you can change, and you can do magical self-esteem-raising work on yourself and be a cool person with an enchanted life. (I am not, by the way, suggesting that the divine Jennifer Lopez is not a real person with sad feelings and bad hair days, just like you or I. It just feels that way.)

True friendship spell

Without really true friends—all types—it's difficult to thrive and take risks with who you are, or even to explore who you want to be. Oh, and without friends, you cut your chances of meeting potential mates. So this spell will help you attract new and magical relationships into your life. If you are really annoyed with a bunch of so-called friends, this spell will help you retrain either them or yourself, and you'll be better pals for it. If you are lonely, this spell will help you to become the social butterfly you should be from time to time.

This spell will:

- Enhance friendships;
- Make you radiate feel-good vibes;
- Help you believe in yourself;
- Assist your ability to say no to greedy vampire friends;
- Help you overcome the fear that you'll die alone and be eaten by your Pekingese; and
- Help you go out and party like it's still 1999!

Bake a cherry cake,
and share it with the friends you wish to nurture.
Before serving,
carve a symbol of love (it can be a heart) into the cake,
And as you taste its flavor,
Know these friendships
will be a part of you,
As long as you remind yourself
to savor their unique qualities.

Now that we've discovered ways of getting more friends who have something to give, let's look at concrete ways to manifest those guys.

First things first. You will never meet anyone watching *Buffy the Vampire Slayer* reruns BY YOURSELF. Did you get those two keywords?

So, if you love Buffy (or Spike, as I do), the thing to do is to invite two girlfriends around to your place, and they have to bring along two friends who you've never met before. What if they're girls, I hear you shrieking.

The point is, the more soul mate girlfriends you have, the more likely you are to meet a great guy—one who doesn't require you to get the secret service to check him out. One who doesn't wear military gear or have a bong in the shape of a dolphin. Are you getting my drift?

Now, if you're the kind of person who freaks out at the idea of inviting people around to do anything, stop now. If you're like me, and just lazy, well, decide what you love. Laziness, or loneliness. Not much of a choice, is it?

Here's a selection of things to do, suitable for at-home teenagers (who're out as much as is legal) as well as hard core thirty-something perma-singles already glimpsing a mid-life tunnel of love crisis:

- Host a video-fest theme night;
- Throw a themed dinner party, the more tragic the better—laughter rules;
- Have a picnic in a beautiful park with gorgeous food;
- Have a tea party;
- Join a soccer or softball team; and
- Rent a space and have a great birthday bash with about three people who share your birth month. This will make you look awesomely confident, and all the friends who come will bring friends, who will bring friends—a virtual man-fest!

So, it's all about connecting through friends. Forget agencies. Forget walking up to gorgeous strangers on the street—unless you're really confident, or have done one mighty self-defense course. Don't crash your car into the car of the hunk in the other lane. Don't pretend to drown at the beach. Do say hello to guys you see around. It doesn't have to be full-on—just a nice hi will do, or a nod, if you think your voice will fail you. You are allowed to flirt, but please avoid coming over all dippy.

You flirty thing

Flirting has many manifestations. Here's some simple flirt magic to start with.

- Hold a copy of *Vogue* and *New Scientist* at the same time;
- Wear some red red lipstick;
- Buy some brand new perfume;
- Dress in pink;
- Coat your lashes with mascara;
- Tilt your chin down, and look upwards;
- Think dirty, and you'll talk flirty; and
- Be smart and funny.

This is a visualization, girls, so set aside some 30 seconds or so when you need it:

Visualize your inner charmer—
she can be a tall, slim,
Miss Sassy Pants—
standing beside you.
Or a teeny va-va-va sex boom-ba kitten
small enough to perch on your shoulder.
But they will be with you,
To inspire you,
And encourage you,
And remind you that you're never alone,
Or at a loss for words,
Because you are never alone with this saucy woman
whispering suggestions in your ear.

Always be true to yourself

Nobody else does you quite so well, so get to know who you are, and work on loving what you find. Everything can be a positive or a negative. People who are sensitive are empaths; people who are emotional are in touch with themselves; people who are cold can be calm and serene. It's all about the spin you give yourself. Talk yourself up—it's your job. If you find things about yourself that you do not like, then work on modifying those aspects into positive manifestations.

Here's a little story about two very famous people that I think is quite sweet (and not because they're famous) and indicative of the need to be true to who you are. Really, truly true to you.

There once was a girl who wasn't a princess, but she was beautiful, and sweet and clever and talented. She grew up and was celebrated everywhere for her beauty, but such was her love of beauty in other things—namely dolphins—that she had an artist draw a picture of twin dolphins on her upper arm as a symbol of her love for her ocean soul mates.

The girl's mother wept and cried: How will you ever meet your prince now that you have blighted your beauty?

But the girl did meet a boy, and he too had carvings on himself. Only he was a prince. As the girl, Sarah O' Hare, says, "When I met Lachlan, he had more tattoos than me."

So if you're thinking of not doing something that feels right, like not getting tattoos because models shouldn't have them, or because you'll never meet someone special if you remain true to yourself, just remember Ms Sarah O'Hare. She got the tatts, and her prince, and who knows, maybe it was those tatts more than anything else that made them recognize each other as soul mates.

The "I will only meet great guys" spell

Men. My place. Now. Cast this spell and you'll be a complete guy magnet.

On a Wednesday,
Light a stick of rose incense.
Take a red heart and place it on a green piece of fabric.
Pick out about three pictures of guys who embody the qualities you want,
and put them on top of the heart.
(Be careful—pick Tom Cruise and you might get a Scientologist.)
Then sew it up into a pouch.
Place this in a magical place.
Light two red candles anointed with jasmine oil
And place them on either side of the pouch.
Concentrate on the heart, and the pictures.
Visualize your dream guys coming into your life—right here, right now.
Say three times:
"As the waves of the ocean are infinite,
And as the trees in the forest grow tall,
So shall my lovers desire me,
I am ready to receive my all."

Shift your focus to the magical pouch and understand that love and lovers are coming your way.

Blow out first the candle on the right then the one on the left, and place flowers and sprigs of fast-growing romantic plants—such as jasmine or roses—around your magical space.

Now watch out on the love horizon for the approach of your sonic-boom lover boy.

At-a-glance magic for attracting guys

Affirmation: "I am never lonely, as I am a loving person who easily attracts other loving people into my life." (Keep repeating that.)

Day of the week: Wednesday—it's all about reaching out.

Colors: Blue, silver, or orange.

Stone: Rhodonite, because its presence maintains glamour, reduces self-doubt, builds confidence, and it's a heart healer.

Drink: Anything with lime—it's uplifting.

Goddess: This has to be Helen of Troy—men chased her to distraction.

Essential oils: Clary sage, lime, and frankincense.

4

Did I just meet Mr. Right? (How to recognize a hot prospect from a not prospect)

How do you know if the guy you just met through your friends is okay? That he's not a lunatic, or a minefield of crazy ex-girlfriends, or riddled with insecurities, or maybe gay, or, or, or . . .

You'll never know unless you give him a go. This doesn't have to be as scary as it sounds—or feels. There's probably a subliminal soundtrack playing in your head all the time when it comes to guys. The volume gets turned up when you meet someone nice. Or horrible. Okay, whenever you meet someone.

This soundtrack has conditioned you to behave in various ways, so you respond to people's looks, habits, clothes, smell and voice in predictable ways because they remind you of things. So you need to make a conscious effort to undo the potential damage of this soundtrack.

Girls who've been through one too many love hassles tend to rely on preconceived judgments, and usually end up rejecting the wrong guys. Stop jumping to conclusions and listen to the signs.

Hot prospects tend to do a few things that make them prime contenders for your heart:

- They express interest in you the person, rather than you, the double-D cup;
- They look you in the eye;
- They contact you—*very* important;
- They act a bit nervous when you go out together;
- They try to impress you (this explains nearly all of that embarrassing behavior);
- They try to meet your friends. Hopefully, they may already know them if you've been successful with the friend of a friend strategy;
- They are kind to animals;
- They generally like women;
- They don't pick arguments, or set you tests or challenges to prove how smart they are;
- They listen;

- They laugh;
- They play;
- They are not addicted to drugs, alcohol or cigarettes (though we'll give them a break on that one—many brilliant people have been known to quit and quit again);
- They have had girlfriends who have lasted for more than a month;
- They do not think girls are sluts;
- They do not think guys who sleep around are champs and role models;
- They are not given to emitting burps or farts in your company too early on (unless you both actually like that sort of thing);
- They are healthy, mentally and physically; and
- If they are damaged, they are working on it.

The inaugural list of big boy no-nos

Here are some big boy no-nos to steer completely clear of. Magic won't work on a loser, whichever way you work the enchantment. If he's any of the following, the chances are he'll be trouble.

- He is damaged but has no idea or no intention of working on it;
- He has a girlfriend or a wife, but is drawn to you. (Translation: he wants someone to desire him, so he can feel special again.);
- He criticizes you. (You don't need to make him feel great by not liking yourself.); and
- He is unfaithful. (You don't need to feel like you're not special—and it will make you feel very un-special.)

Signs to foretell future happiness

Are you happy or just relieved when you meet a guy who might be right? Now, you need to ask yourself some questions here.

How much do you like this guy? Him, mind you, not the state of having a date after all this time. It is fine, just fine, to enjoy going out with someone—it's romantic, it's beautiful, it can make both of you feel great. But there is a serious agenda lurking behind the innocent "movie and a quick meal afterwards," and "wanna have a coffee" get-togethers. This is the business of love.

You must not use your powers of attraction to have someone fall in love with you just so you can feel hot. It's great if someone likes you. You are not responsible if they like you a whole lot more than you like them. But you are responsible if you start acting out a love affair with someone you know you're just practicing on. This is not being fair—to you or him—and you can just bet it's going to go wrong somewhere. Wouldn't it be worth keeping it cool and friendly, and getting to meet more men through this guy anyway? If you come over all 'I love you' when you know it's just the worst kind of wishful thinking, you can bet you'll be breaking up in six to eighteen months time and it will all end in tears.

Feeling good about yourself is a top priority of magic, so please be honest. Take things slowly, check your emotional pulse and be aware that when anything starts, it's natural and understandable that you want it to work, but it's okay for it not to work with every guy.

However, it's not okay to jump into messy long-term relationships because you think it's better than being alone. If you are still unhappily single, go back and read some more about friends and then go back and do the spells properly, like you should have the first time. You won't be lonely—just kind of quietly yearning for true love. Which is fine. It will come.

What if he has a girlfriend or is married? Forget it—please. Unless he does the right thing and breaks up with her to pursue his interest in you. It's not okay for him to string either of you along just because he wants everything. Yuck. Greedy. Go away. It's also karmic backlash material—remember the law of the threefold return. And beyond that, it's also about being a goddess. Would you want a ruthless vixen targeting your man? I didn't think so.

How to resist a cool bad guy

There's a dangerous breed of men and women out there. But as we're interested in the men, here it goes. There are the cool guys you want, but who you know are danger on legs. They are:

- Guys who do drugs;
- Guys who do your friends;
- Guys who are charismatic philanderers;
- Guys who involve you in dangerous behavior;
- Guys whose threatening behavior turns you on;
- Guys who are married;
- Guys who care more about their friends and their sexual score cards than they ever would about you—a woman who deserves and will get, believe me, much much better; and
- Guys who wear leather jackets and ride a motorbike. (Okay, it's a stereotype, but you know what I mean.)

Your particular masculine nemesis could wear a suit and tie, and get on like a house on fire with your mother. The thing to remember is that you should never, under any circumstances, have a relationship with anyone who makes you feel bad about yourself. That's a rule, by the way.

But how do you prevent this from happening? Simple. Carry a talisman. It can be a picture of your ideal man, a badge swearing eternal love, or a brooch with an all-seeing eye of Isis on it . . . but give yourself a magical head start when it comes to kicking a bad habit. Bad boys are not worth it. If you must indulge, rent all of the James Dean, Marlon Brando and Mickey Rourke movies you can get your hands on and use your imagination. Then get real.

What if he loves me, but he's just not ready for a commitment right now?

He's either a bit all over the candy store, or he's actually not that interested, but trying to have you hang in there in case he changes his mind. Yuck. Guys like that should just go away.

Mr. Walking Wounded

Mr. Walking Wounded is such a pain. Usually, he's just using the "I'm still not over her" line to make himself seem more interesting. If you genuinely believe that he truly isn't over someone, give him a very wide love berth. Don't play the old ego game of "I can make him forget her." You can't—only he can.

Mr. Wow, this just might go somewhere I feel like staying for a while

He's nice, and makes you feel like a fine and attractive person when you're with him. He laughs with you, not at you. He's single and may be looking, though he's not too obvious about it. He doesn't act like he's a lone wolf à la Clint Eastwood, either. He behaves like himself. Sometimes he gets a bit nervous, or he's a bit scruffy (or exceptionally gorgeous—it's not really about appearance). He's not perfect, but he's nice. You feel good after you've seen him, you wouldn't have to get drunk to kiss him.

At-a-glance magic to distinguish good men from bad.

Affirmation: "All my relationships are working for my highest good. I know I am divinely protected and loved."

Day of the week: Tuesday, for when emotions are clear and you're able to do some hard thinking.

Color: Blue, for clarity in decision making.

Stone: Clear quartz crystal for power and level-headedness.

Drink: Spring water for its cleansing powers.

Goddess: Diana, the huntress, for ruthless honesty in sizing him up.

Essential oil: Bergamot, for protection.

Herb: Feverfew, to clear your thoughts.

5

First date trauma (Have you got the nerve?)

So, you've established he might be a Mr. Wow. Now comes the hardest part: going on your first date. First dates are meant to be exciting and dreadful. They may go right, they may go wrong, but, whatever happens, remember that it's pretty brave of you to go in the first place. Don't let first date jitters ruin your night. Hopefully you've seen him in action when you were less interested in each other, so you've got some idea of what he's like. *Now for the showdown.* Deep breath . . . exhale . . . Okay, let's get moving.

Where should you go?

This depends on your feelings, his feelings and what's been happening between you. If you've been making gooey eyes at each other for weeks, go for a romantic night together. Get into it. But don't get completely trashed and wake up next to him even if you're convinced that he's "the one." Take your time and don't rush things.

Here are some ideas for your first date:

- You could go somewhere neutral, like out for a coffee;
- See a film together, but be warned! Films tend to point out essential boy-girl differences, which could be perceived as incompatibilities;
- Go to a football game, but only if it's special to him and crowds excite you;
- Have a drink at a bar, but don't get trashed. It's hard to keep that ooey-gooey thing going when you haven't got sunglasses and you're wearing a party dress on Pitt Street at 8:00 a.m. on a Saturday morning; or
- Go on a picnic. This could be romantic if he is the sweet guy you thought he was, or just public enough for him to keep his hands to himself if he turns out to be a dud.

Where not to go

- A club, a demolition derby, a zoo, out to score drugs (it happens!), or to dinner at a posh place if you hardly know each other;
- A home dinner. Great idea, but not on a first date—too much pressure on you to perform in the kitchen—and anyway, no-one can eat if they're falling in love;
- A friend's wedding. If you're over thirty, great. If 20-something, way too scary—he might think you're trying to tell him something;
- For a walk. Are you both insane? You're too young to be wearing comfortable shoes, surely;
- To the beach. At least you get to check out the goods, but if you're extremely self-conscious forget it; or
- Meeting you after work, or picking you up at the office. No way. What if he turns out to be a stalker—then he'll know where you work. Eek!

Staying safe on first dates (or any dates) spell

The thrill of a first encounter can be tinged with panic as sheer as your best seamless stockings. Don't go all Bambi on me—cast this spell and head out with confidence.

If you are going out with a new man,
The night before your date,
Go to your magical space,
Take a few moments to clear your mind,
Then breathe in blue light.
Take a silver ribbon,

And wrap it between your fingers,
Forming a star on the back of your hand.
Then, in a blue pouch,
Place:
One sea shell,
Leaves from a lemon tree,
And some earth from your home
(soil from a pot plant will do if you don't have a yard).

Sleep with the silver ribbon around your wrist and carry the talisman in your handbag, and you'll get home safely.

Keeping your life and home safe and lovely spell

Having a safe home makes you feel secure. It's your nest where you return to freshen up for your forays into the world of relationship-hunting. A safe, happy home is to be treasured—never take it, or your lovely roomies, for granted. They are the new family.

To protect your home,
Visualize a circle of white light
around your house.
See this magical circle radiating out,
So that every part of your home—
Every window,
Every door,
From above,
And below—
Is protected by this divine white light.

Then, when leaving home,
Draw a star in your mind's eye over the front and back doors,
Again in white.
Your home will be:
Spiritually,
Magically,
Actually,
Secure.

He thinks you're beautiful spell

And then, the dream we all dream of. Oh, to be gorgeous, or at least to make everyone think you are. Oh, how wonderful it would be to tumble out of bed with glorious hair, fresh eyes and sweet-scented breath. Hmm. I'm sure we could all do with a little magic here.

The secret is, no matter how gorgeous someone is—think Hollywood, think star, think the best plastic surgeon ever—nobody feels beautiful all the time. It sounds like a crock, but there is not a single woman alive who cannot ooze goddessness once they start to shine from the inside.

Being beautiful is a result of believing in the beauty that already exists within you. So the trick with this spell is that it will fuse your inner and outer beauty, creating one big gorgeous you.

On a Friday night, with a waxing moon,
Pour a bath into which a spoon,
Of jasmine flowers have been strewn,
Gaze upon your body divine.
See its perfection,
Make it shine.

Cleanse your perfection,
Banish ill-thought,
Forget every negative
You have been taught.
Because you are beautiful,
Because you're sublime,
Because you deserve
To know you're divine.

Do this every Friday night when the moon waxes, and you will feel and look as you truly are—gaspingly gorgeous.

At-a-glance magic for first dates

Affirmation: "I welcome the opportunity to spend time with guys who could be great for me."

Day of the week: Friday, but the date call should be booked on Wednesday (Mercury—communication).

Color: Ivory—it's very flattering to nearly all skin-tones.

Stone: Diamond—wear one for sparkle.

Drink: Semillon—clean, elegant, sexy and fragrant.

Goddess: Aphrodite—you may as well be hopeful and go for the goddess with the mostest.

Essential oils: Jasmine blended with bergamot (making you lovely and protected).

Herb: Calendula will encourage you to hold back a little, without diminishing your allure.

6

First sex trauma (We just did it—are we ever going to get over it?)

Oh goodness me. First sex, like first dates, can be oh so hard. It's not easy to have great intimacy with someone who you're excited by—because excitement makes us eager, clumsy, funny and beautifully human. The best first-time sex philosophy is to hope for a great time, laughter, snuggles and maybe, just maybe, if Aphrodite's having a good day in the cosmic office—simultaneous orgasm.

This could get real, as in forever, now, so it's time to assess.

Like a virgin—again

First time sex with anyone is a little like rediscovering your emotional virginity, so if you're doing it with someone you care for and think there may be a hint of "forever" on the horizon, it can be very very scary indeed. You may have already worked out your sexual style, and now here comes Mr. Maybe to throw a wrench in the works. You'll need to be flexible—and I don't mean that literally (though you can add that to the list if you wish).

And if changing your sexual style wasn't enough, you may have to rewrite or rework his. However, the thing to fear the most, girls, is seeing his bedroom.

What am I saying? Well, sometimes a boy's sleeping quarters are virtually signs of arrested development. But don't jump to conclusions—your man's boudoir could be a bachelor sanctuary. Just prepare yourself for the worst—grubby Salvation Army sheets and pillowcases, and threadbare nylon covers. Yes, boys sometimes just don't get their act together on the interior decoration front. Does this make him a candidate for rejection, or just friendship? That depends.

Suspect bedroom paraphernalia:
- Toy soldiers;
- 100 per cent unwashed nylon sheets;
- Hundreds of photographs of another woman;
- More than one framed photograph of his mom;
- Maps of the world's trouble spots;
- Stuffed toys (we're talking possible plushies);

- Hundreds of family-sized condom packs;
- Used condoms by the bed;
- Girly posters; or
- Eminem posters.

If you've known this man for a while, he's had every opportunity to clear up his bedroom act. So if he hasn't changed the sheets, cleaned the floor, removed the skidmarked undies or evidence of other women, he just isn't trying hard enough.

Should you do it at home, or should it be an away game

This depends on many factors.

Advantages to an away game
- You have a quick escape route;
- You can control the damage;
- You get to see what his personality is like at home;
- You get to check out his roommates;
- You can see if his towels are clean; and
- You'll see what sort of breakfasts he offers.

Disadvantages
- Not knowing whether you've overstayed your welcome;
- His roommates have ears, and eyes; and
- The obligatory skimpy-towelled dash to the toilet through the gross living room, which is full of his sleeping roommates.

Advantages to an at-home game
- You'll feel more comfy;
- No dashes to the bathroom (*he* has to make the dash);
- Your sheets are nicer;
- A bathroom full of girly things to repair bedroom hair and morning-after makeup mess;

- A loyal cheering squad of wonderful roommates; and
- If it wasn't that great, you can quickly consult this book.

And the disadvantages . . .
- Your roommates, if they are nosy;
- He might stay, and stay, and stay . . .
- He might bolt; and
- Eek! Now he knows where you live.

What if something embarrassing happens?

Get over it—the whole thing about sex is that we overcome something embarrassing because it's so beautiful and gorgeous to have physical communion with someone. If it isn't easy to get over noises and strange smells, you're not going to be able to handle intimacy.

What if I think a bit of his body is weird? Everybody's body is weird—unless you're talking about something like an extra arm, which is another thing altogether.

What if we have the best sex ever and then we break up? There's always that chance. At least you'll have upped your standards. Just remember that nobody, not even you, comes with a guarantee.

Passionate first night spell

This should guarantee you a hot first sex marathon—not perfect, but with genuine erotic potential, and enough frisson to ensure you'll ditzily giggle about for the next week . . .

*On a Friday
During a waxing moon,
Take a silver pin and*

Carve your boyfriend's name, entwined with your own,
Into a crimson candle.
Anoint your candle with seven drops of rose oil,
And seven drops of jasmine oil.
Light the candle at 7.00 p.m., for seven minutes, for seven nights.
Scatter the wax in moving water,
And as it moves away,
See it as if it is the two of you, lovers, now on your romantic journey together.
And with this visualization to bind it,
This spell's power to create love Threefold, will return to you.

If there is no one in your life at the moment, or if you do not want to be specific because you've got so many boys on the boil, simply carve the word "beloved" into your candle—or Ewan McGregor, or whatever you want. If you ask for it, the Goddesses will all unite and send an absolutely gorgeous boy-band lookalike for you to enjoy.

Sea Siren Seductress

So, you know tonight's the night. You're waxed, perfumed, be-corsetted. Call on the sea sirens to help you sex-kitten your way to ultimate enjoyment.

When the moonlight is strong,
Move in its rays,
And sing these words softly
Three times before day:
"My one true love,
I draw to me

With the magic of the sea,
And by the power of three times three
As I do wish, so mote it be."
Place an image of a mermaid (the local aquarium should have many.
I purchased mine for $3.95, and she is delightful!)
In a place where you can see her every day,
So that her vivacity can inspire you to be more and more who you
truly are.

The morning after

There's got to be a morning after—scary, huh? There are two major dilemmas to face up to here.

1. Nerves

After first time sex you will be sick with nerves, then high on the excitement of possibility, then back to being sick with nerves. Ain't love grand?

2. Will he call?

Make this conundrum redundant and e-mail him first. Try not to come across like a stalker. Acknowledge the night. If he doesn't answer, either his connection's gone down, or your relationship has. He knows where you live—especially if he stayed overnight.

If you don't want him to call, rub your phone with some fresh garlic. And, if you do, anoint the phone with rose oil—he'll be calling before you know it.

At-a-glance magic for the debut sex stress

Affirmation: "My first night with my new man will be romantic and exciting."

Days of the week: Saturday and Sunday.

Color: Black, as in big black sunglasses—great for wearing on your way home . . .

Stone: Aquamarine will banish fears, aid self-expression and inspire calm.

Drink: One shot of vodka for confidence.

Goddesses: Kwan Yin, the goddess of mercy and Eartha Kitt (for sex kitten magic incarnate).

Essential oil: Ylang ylang, for its hypnotic qualities.

Herb: The delicious, sexy fig.

7

Are we going out yet? (That strange in-between relationship time we all know and love to hate)

The time between the first date and the second and third times you see each other can be, in a word, hell. While it's exciting and thrilling, it's a time of tension and uncertainty as you wait for text messages, e-mails or phone calls—or nervously make them yourself. This is the establishment time of your relationship. You're both showing interest in each other, but all the time you're assessing one thing: is this worth pursuing?

When you first start out, there's so much to think about. And that includes the fact that women these days feel quite pressured to get sexually intimate before they've even figured out whether they like the guy.

Which is just the way it is: but darn hard if, after you've slept with him, you discover he's got major issues with employment or women, or a hankering for stamp collecting, or taking photos of you when you're asleep and posting them on a website he's developed devoted totally to you . . .

There are endless hassles at this stage, so what you need is some magical help to slow down and let the rest of your life work while you're obsessing about the "maybe" stage of this relationship.

How will I know? spell

How will you know if he's right for you—if he's the one man you're never going to wash right out of your hair? Here's how you'll know . . .

On the Tuesday night
Of a new moon,
Gather, in a scrap of red velvet,
A pinch of:
Green tea,
Sea salt,
One sprig of rosemary,

And several cloves.
Wearing a silver thimble,
Stitch the velvet into a pouch,
With turquoise thread.
Keep it under your pillow.
Your strength will build,
As the fragrance of this magical pouch fades.

Get up off that couch and ask him what's happening spell

Relationship angst. It's *so* not done for a girl to make the faintest shimmy toward clarifying the relationship puzzle. All that silence when we need to ask important questions can make a magic girl feel like her inner-goddess has melted down, like she has no vital va-va-va-voom left. Now you need to get out and amongst it all. Here's how to take your place as one of life's bombshells, and his number one girl.

Monday morning
After a new moon,
Juice an orange
In the sunlight.
Place in a glass,
With freshly grated ginger
And drink immediately.
Repeat every morning for a week.
Go barefoot as often as you can,
Go ankle deep in sea water,
And bathe in sunshine.

Flirty-skirty spell

Oh boy. Flirting's bad, isn't it? It can get you into some serious trouble. Well, not if you do it properly. You don't have to bat your eyelids so it looks like your contact lense has slipped, and you certainly don't have to drop your IQ either. Rather, make physical contact that's unthreatening but clear in its intent and make meaningful eye contact. Just remember that there's no commitment to flirting, that's why it's so great. A man may flirt with you without actually being seriously interested, too. It's all about testing the water, and you have to do that unless you're a fan of the arranged marriage.

Flirting makes you feel happy, when it's done right. It makes you believe in your attractiveness. There's nothing like that little flame of interest in a new hunk's eyes to make you believe you still have some mojo, after all. It's the magical power that enables you to laugh and dance. Joy is a bubbling over of divine happiness, a dip into the cosmic well of hope and freedom. When you are joyful you are divine—and magic worked to experience joy more often is sacred, powerful and a wonder of the Universe.

Take nine drops of rose oil,
Some jasmine tea,
Nine silver-colored coins,
Three pink candles,
A silver-colored bowl,
And a silver pouch.
As a waxing moon on a Sunday night is rising,
Blend the rose and almond oil together and rub the mixture slowly all over your body.
Slowly drink a cup of jasmine tea, and place the nine coins into a silver bowl. Take the bowl outside and place it under the moonlight.

After one hour, bring the bowl back in and place the coins into the silver pouch.
Next to the pouch, light the three pink candles (be sure to keep an eye on them, as you don't want to set anything alight).
Let them burn down completely.
Take the wax and bury it in the earth with one of the silver coins.
And know that what you think of, and what you do, will return to you, With the power of three times three.

The next date you have, make it dinner at your place. Wear a scarlet, black or silver slip dress—no underwear. Then ask him what's going on.

At-a-glance magic for girls on the verge of a relationship

Affirmation: "I am lovable and loving. I welcome romance into my life."

Day of the week: Sunday, especially if you're spending it together.

Colors: White, red, pink and peach.

Stone: Jasper—it'll make you friendly but feisty.

Drink: Afternoon cups of tea spell togetherness.

Goddesses: Lauren Bacall, Scarlett O'Hara, Kim Cattrall, Demeter (goddess of reaping what you've sown), Bridget Jones and Selene (goddess of the moon).

Essential oils: Cedarwood, Frankincense, lime, and rose.

Herb: Rose—for love, of course.

8

I'm seeing someone (Why guys are weird around your friends)

There are some very important people in your life—there are mentors and teachers who've shone a light into the dark corners of your career wilderness, and there are people who've encouraged and believed in you even when you thought they must be sorely deluded. Then there are friends. True friends. The ones who have been on the end of the phone when the break-up has been so bad you've contemplated calling a shrink. And you probably know you should always stay in touch with your girlfriends, no matter what happens to any of your love lives.

Hmm. I'm going to get all realistic here. Yes, your girlfriends are truly important, but change is inevitable, which isn't such a bad thing. You can't remain in a state of suspended friendship animation with all of you single and loving it forever. Life, as well as your wardrobe, is sadly not like *Sex and the City*.

Here comes the truth. Put your sunglasses on . . .

Having a new boyfriend will change your friendships.

You can only hope that ultimately your single friends will meet a Mr. Maybe of their very own, if that's what they want.

But what you do hope will work, and what you do have to reconcile yourself to putting lots of effort into, is the fact that these very important people in your life will meet up and may or may not get along. More than likely not get along. Guys, in particular, are not usually that great at that blending with the friendship thing.

Friends usually have the perfect man in mind for you, an ideal man that they've made up for themselves based on all your years of pining after seemingly unobtainable hunks, bad boys, or musicians with no money (or scruples). They thought you'd end up with a rock star, a doctor, or an Academy Award-winning actor. Your version of Mr. Right may actually look quite average in their eyes.

The day will come when he finally meets your friends, and he gets a severe dose of performance anxiety. He may stutter, mumble and find it difficult to make eye contact. He may even come across like a serial killer's apprentice. And you're sitting there wondering where that clever, funny, handsome man's gone.

Then if your girlfriends who love you don't approve, or don't find him as attractive as do you, you may start to see him through the prism of their unforgiving gaze. Ditto for him, if he thinks they're a pack of bitches. For you, it can be really hard dealing with the great loyalty divide once it happens.

The reason this may happen is because girlfriends worry that you might not have time for them any more. And, more than likely, they are trying to protect you and don't want to see you get hurt. Boyfriends worry because your girlfriends might turn you against him.

You need to read both of them the friendship charter of independence and commitment below.

Magic girl's Friendship Declaration of Love and Independence

I am your friend, until further notice, forever.
I know our friendship will endure through many changes.
I love you and promise to stay in touch,
But you've got to cut me some slack while I am in the love zone.
I understand that my prince may look like a frog to you.
I don't expect you to adore him like I do.
But giving him at least three chances is part of the deal,
And I promise to do the same for you,
No matter how much I may want to scream "dump and run" at you.
Your friend,
Magic girl.

To him, this applies as well.

Magic girl's Boyfriend Declaration of Love and Independence

I know it can be acutely weird and embarrassing meeting my gal pals,
Who are likely to bite you if you put a foot wrong.

I know they can make you feel like you are Mr. Wrong personified.
I do not expect you to fit in immediately,
But it would be great if we could eventually hang out from time to time,
In a relaxed kind of way.
I love you for now, and maybe for a much longer time,
And you have my loyalty.
I won't choose,
And I will hang with them,
But I love you and you're my man.
Love,
Magic girl.

How to conjure up a boyfriend/girlfriend merger and acquisition

So, to spellwork. One of the best and most sensible approaches to the meet and greet is to just hang at home. Burn bergamot—it's a friendly, chatty oil. Plunk lots of rose quartz in unseen places, and cook something that is sweet and friendly. It sounds really corny, but re-enacting a kid's birthday party can be a good idea. (Not too much alcohol. If people are tense, awkward behavior could become an issue.)

Scratch a message into some cupcakes or pigs-in-a-blanket. This will make everyone feel lovely and child-like, just like you were back in the days when you were little and everyone felt they always had room for at least one more best friend. Plant ideas in your friends' minds with these little cupcakes, like you and Mr. X get on well—but not too well. You accept my choices, and love me. You like my friends and get along well with them. Get munching!

Or you could just pop words like *joy, companionship, laughter, cheer, harmony,* and *friendship* into the goodies.

You don't have to spend hours laboring over long sentences. Just include the vibe you want to spread—even a smiley face or a little heart will do, and then pass those munchies around.

As you heat up the goodies, see your wishes heating up and taking life. If you've fallen out with a friend over your new relationship, get two empty tubes (toilet rolls devoid of toilet paper will be fine—you'll find plenty of those at your boyfriend's place). Use a blue pen to write you and your friends' names on the outside of the tube. Then cover the bottom of the tube with your hand. Sprinkle sugar (for sweetness), salt (for cleansing), and flour (for growth) in the top of the tube. Shake it up, and visualize your friendship healing itself and improving. Visualize communicating with this person—it could be just sending an e-mail, or getting a phone call. Just think good thoughts about them, and in one moon's time things will have turned around.

At-a-glance magic for friends and boyfriend mergers

Affirmation: "Those who I love now love each other."

Day of the week: Friday nights.

Color: Rose.

Stone: Amethyst, for creativity, social skills, and easy laughter.

Drink: Red wine, for its anti-oxidants and social lubrication.

Goddesses: The "Sex and the City" girls, the "Friends" friends, Xena and Gabrielle, Marilyn Monroe and Jane Russell.

Essential oils: Lemon, lemon verbena, and lemon myrtle.

Herb: Rosemary—eat plenty of it for wisdom.

9

The call of the wild (Getting along with his horrible friends)

*A*nd then there may be the night when you're introduced to his friends. If he's clever he'll keep them (the nights, not his friends) to a minimum. It's not always nice to meet a whole bunch of curious guys when you're having sex with their buddy. You know they're all checking you out, wondering what you look like naked, and you're probably outnumbered as well as nervous.

Then may come the nights when he wants to go out with the boys. Fine. You like hanging with your friends. It's imperative, and you need to see them on your own so you can talk about him. But he needs to be with his pals alone so he can re-enact moments of the boyhood you've never ever caught glimpses of.

Some of the activities likely to be incorporated into a great boy's night out could include:

- Chugging beer;
- Throwing empty beer cans at the television set when their team loses due to a totally unfair call from a biased referee;
- Dancing to "Eye of the Tiger";
- Ogling babes;
- Chugging more beer;
- Throwing up;
- Arriving home really drunk and babbling about Bluey and Joe being great buddies;
- Waking you up to come meet Bluey and Joe, who are in the living room, and will still be there in the morning and all of the next day;
- Going out and not coming home . . . for days; and
- Going out and not coming home, then calling you from somewhere else entirely—like Boston, when you live in New York—and asking for you to come get him and the boys.

Basically, his friends can help thrust your relationship into a zone best known as the horrible pre-feminist '70s nightmare.

Banish those unwanted bodies in the living room spell

Sprinkle a small amount of pepper and vinegar across the doorstep when your beloved goes with the boys for a night of rampage. This will stop his buddies from following him home, so you won't have to compete with them for his time, affection and loyalty. Go to the back door, and sprinkle some more. Say aloud:

*"I am queen here—this is my house.
My beloved may enter, but others
return home."*

You'll be surprised how many of your guy's friends find girlfriends after this little spell.

Unfair tactics spell

This spell will make him wonder what he was doing, running around with his friends when he could have been snuggling up to sexy you . . .

*Take one black negligee,
One bottle of French champagne,
One bowl of strawberries,
One dollop of cream,
One sexy music track,
One squirt of your favorite perfume, and*

One technique from the Kamasutra.
Feed boyfriend, to the music, on the floor.
Kiss him holding his head in your hands.
Eat the mixture from his body, then head to the tub together...

Yes, he'll make those nights out just a little fewer.

At-a-glance magic for dealing with the friends

Affirmation: "My home is my sanctuary—I will protect it."

Day of the week: Tuesday, for courage and energy during the talk you're going to have with your guy.

Color: Chocolatey browns, for soothing his nerves and keeping you grounded.

Stone: Gold, for wisdom and belief in yourself.

Drink: Earl Grey tea—the bergamot will protect you and heighten your powers of persuasion.

Goddess: Cerridwen—for real wisdom.

Essential oil: Clary sage, for respect.

Herb: Witch hazel!

10

Sex hassles
(How to avoid the
daily bump 'n' grind)

Oh my god.
   That was truly the worst sex you've ever had, wasn't it?
   And if it wasn't, I don't even want to hear about the other bad sex you've had—that time must've been awful.

Oh, but this *was* bad. Undeniably. Even counting all those behind-the-bus-stop fumblings with boys your own age when you were . . . oh, never mind.

I don't care if he's got money, treats you nice, opens the Porsche door for you, and has a summer house on the Vineyard. Hmmm. A summer house. (I mean, could it have been that bad?—yes, yes, yes it was.)

And he does have a hot car. Could you have hallucinated the whole thing? (No, because there he is, next to you, and there you are, already dressed and slipping away for, um, an early morning jog . . .)

Bad sex with a person you just don't find physically attractive is a big waste of time and an insult to all the beauty and wonder and damn good fun of good sex with someone you want to touch, smell and feel again and again under your fingers.

Bad sex is an insult to your body and your mind. Trust your instincts. It doesn't matter that he took you shopping, really it doesn't. That's nice, but you're never going to want to take those clothes off, and that's what counts.

Next you run through the list of typically female self-persecuting questions, like:

- Perhaps you put him off his game (yeah, right, it's how you gave it your best shot that really repulsed him);
- Maybe he wasn't feeling well (which is why he wanted to keep going and going and going and, oh, God);
- Maybe he didn't find you attractive (so how did you end up naked then?).
- Could he have been just really nervous?
- Inexperienced?
- Bad at sex?

Whatever. If it was that awful, do both of you a big favor and drop this one in the box marked, "Gee, that was interesting, but I'm not sure I'm looking for a relationship right now."

There are some things that work on a very magical, visceral, sub-atomic level, and you just shouldn't mess with that sort of pheromonal juju if happiness is truly what you're after. I mean, you may be fretting, but someone else will find the guy you can't stand in bed a Love God. Yes, they will. And that's a wonderful thing. For them and for you.

The Is there chemistry? quiz

1. He smiles, and you:
    a. get butterflies in your tummy.
    b. feel nauseous.
    c. worry that this means he likes you.
2. He yawns and you:
    a. worry you've bored him.
    b. think, awww, he's tired.
    c. hold your nose.
3. He tickles you and you:
    a. squeal with delight.
    b. run away, refusing to come out of the bathroom till he leaves the house.
    c. sob hysterically or throw up.
4. His hand traces a path up your skirt and you:
    a. go straight home and change into pants.
    b. slap him really hard.
    c. jump up and run to the toilet (to throw up).
5. He smells:
    a. delicious—especially when he's got that funky underarm thing happening.
    b. like he could wash a little more.
    c. yes, he does.

What it means:

Simple. Mostly A's—you're in heaven. Mostly B's—it's not the perfect relationship, but it's okay. Mostly C's—have a bit of respect and clear out of there immediately.

How to improve a B-grade lover

A natural A-man doesn't need help. A C-boy isn't going to be around for long, but B, well B-guys you can work on with the following va-va-va-boom chemistry tricks.

You have to be a love coach. Come on, you have to, even if the whole idea makes you squirm. Do it for the B-guy—you just might turn him into the A-man you've been waiting for.

This courage is what separates the women from the Barbie dolls amongst us.

Take control of your sexual happiness, and try these aphrodisiacs to promote sensuality and love. It is okay to acknowledge areas in your life that need work. You deserve a truly erotic love life.

Affirmation:

"I now can enjoy erotic experiences without feeling emotionally attached. I can walk away, even after sex that is great. I know it is best to have a great memory of several nights than a bad relationship. I now know that great relationships with fabulous sex are possible."

Top 10 aphrodisiacs
- Basil can be rubbed on your lover if you fear him straying. Eat some pasta off his body, topped with basil, for the ultimate plan in keeping him from straying—he'll never want to.
- Cardamom is a traditional Indian herbal remedy for men's staying power problems. Boil the seeds in milk to treat impotence and premature ejaculation. Hmm. Just say it's chai tea, and see the love action that results.
- Chocolate contains the chemical phenylethylamine, which stimulates the nervous system and gives a feeling of bliss. It does this by

encouraging your body to pump out endorphins, or happy hormones, leaving you feeling high on life and love.

- Cloves help digestion and promote male desire. They've been used in potions in Asia since around 3 BC. Many centuries later in Europe, Swedish herbalist Anders Mansson Rydaholm wrote: "If a man loses his ability, he should stay sober and drink milk spiced with five grams of cloves. This will fortify him and make him desire his wife."
- Figs are sacred to Dionysus, the god of sex and revelry. As the legend goes, he offered them to Priapus, the god of long, hard, sustained nights of passion.
- Honey strengthens and lengthens any love spell or potion. For amazing effect, try manuka honey—its healing and antibacterial properties are legendary.
- Hops, found in beer, are good news for women, as they stimulate the sex hormone estrogen. So a glass or two a day is great for girls, but can lead to lousy performances between the sheets for men. It's said to be one of the main reasons for what's called "brewer's droop."
- Oysters are a famous aphrodisiac—they're packed with zinc, which is a trace mineral vital for men's reproductive health. For women, the effect is to be more sensitive to the touch—your skin feels extra alive after eating oysters. They also help get rid of gas, which is not sexy.
- Tomatoes are an excellent aphrodisiac, which may be linked to the fact that they are particularly good for men's sexual health—the chemical lycopene, released when a tomato is cooked, protects men from prostate cancer.
- Truffles are extremely sexy, perhaps because their scent is similar to the male pheromone androsterone. They are extremely expensive, but then throwing money around on sexy food can be quite arousing, too.

At-a-glance magic for turning him into a love god

Affirmation: "I now can enjoy erotic experiences. I now know that great relationships with fabulous sex are possible."

Day of the week: Friday, as it's Aphrodite's day, and she's very saucy.

Colors: Pink, red, scarlet, crimson—anything the color of blood, roses, and red, red wine.

Stones: Rubies and antique jewelry.

Drink: Mead (red wine with cloves).

Goddess: Persephone, the goddess who turned a kidnapping into an opportunity.

Essential oils: Ylang ylang, rose, and jasmine.

Herb: Basil, for concentration.

11

Hex that ex
(Why she must be banished for good)

*F*or many girls, this one's a doozy. The ex. She rings, she visits, she drops in, she wants to stay friends. Maybe not that bad, huh? Maybe she's just at parties, or in the gang. If she's somewhere else, like another country, it's usually somewhere with a great name, like Paris. She writes letters, dropping hints about the emotions that she still has for the guy who's now yours. What do you do? First, let's get some perspective.

Ex-girlfriends who hang on are your boyfriend's barnacles. You can't really stop her altogether, but you do have to look objectively at what's really going on, rather than just reacting when you feel threatened. And threatened is not a bad way to feel. It drives you to take action.

There are two possible problems to face. One, that you are jealous when you have no need to be, and this jealousy could hurt you, your man and your love. Or maybe he has yet to realize the definition of an ex is just that—someone who used to be, not someone who still is.

For the purposes of this chapter, we'll believe you when you say you're not jealous. Rather, she's hovering, and you can't move forward while he's looking over his shoulder at her big moo-cow eyes. Here's how to change things—for the very very better.

Reasons for exes haunting your love zone

First of all, an ex-girlfriend is an ex-girlfriend. (Ditto for an ex-wife, but way more complex if he has children. You're just going to have to accept that if he has kids, there's a link there that cannot be broken. You must find a sensible way to deal with things . . .) For the moment, we'll imagine she's an ex with no children (and if there are little babies involved, what are you even thinking, being involved with him in the first place?). She belongs in the past. If your man has her in his present, there are generally a few explanations for this. Some are acceptable. Some are not.

Excuse 1. He's human, he loves to be loved.
He can't help it if she still loves him and can't let go. After all, he can't hurt her by cutting off contact altogether, can he?

Number one isn't really fair. We all long to be loved, but we have to be true. There's no good in letting others hang on when there's no hope, just an empty space inside you that they conveniently fill for a little bit. That applies to you and your exes, too, by the way.

Savvy solution: State the obvious. Tell it as you see it. If he admits to unfulfilled yearnings, wish him well and move on.

Magical help: Burn the essential oil of bergamot for seven days and tell him goodbye on a Friday, if you can. That weekend will be the worst, so you'll heal faster. Never let the love linger for the entire weekend—it's too painful to look at Monday after you've had goodbye sex. Friday belongs to Aphrodite, and she'll make it easier on you to mourn, move on and meet another guy.

Excuse 2. She either doesn't know about you, or about the seriousness of the relationship.
So she's hanging in there, thinking there's an opportunity—and he's letting her think that. Hmmm. Very interesting . . .

Well, first of all, why doesn't she know about you? She should, if they're still in buddy contact.

Savvy solution: Discover why she doesn't know by asking him. Ask her, if you must. It's your life, not his to play with.

Magical help: The truth is usually told if you're sharing something. So cook him a meal, and while preparing it say this three times:

> *"As you eat my bread*
> *And drink my wine,*
> *You cannot hold back*
> *What must be mine:*
>   *The truth,*
>   *The truth,*
>   *The truth."*

Then tell him how much you trust him, and ask the question. If it feels right, fine. If you're still twitching, send him home, break out the chocolate and play sad songs till you're over him.

Excuse 3. He's still sleeping with her.
I mean, why not? It does no-one any harm, he's going to stop just as soon as he thinks of a way to tell the ex he has a new girlfriend.

Savvy solution: If you discover this is the case, you've got to go. Don't wait to collect $200, just send him straight to love jail, lock the door behind him and throw away the key. That sort of behavior shows that he has major self-esteem issues, especially if he needs all that attention and drama to make him feel okay. Let him grow up in the space that you leave him with. You won't help him or yourself by staying there.

Go now. No, not after you've spoken and given him another chance. Go now!

Magical help: Courage essential oil by Sunspirit is beautiful, strengthening, and gives you the determination to move on. You're leaving a no-win love situation. Take a rose quartz stone, place it in your pocket, and think of him with the kind of love that's from a distance. In your mind's eye, see him becoming smaller and smaller—literally wave goodbye if you wish. This isn't about anger, it's about leaving. So say goodbye kindly and move on.

How to find out if he's double dipping . . .

Chant this to yourself for focus, courage and de-steaming if you're all worked up

> *"The truth—so shall it be told,*
> *The truth—before it is too old,*
> *The truth—or else I shall grow cold."*

Make a yummy dinner, toss red fabric over his chair when you sit down to eat. Ask him what's going on after dinner. Make a lot of eye contact, and don't lose your temper.

If he tells you the truth, and it feels right, break out a block of chocolate, say a little thankyou, silently, and share it to bind your trust. If he lies, go cold as the ice cream you're going to be eating alone later—and ask him to leave. Tell him you're suddenly not feeling very well (and the thing that's making you sick are lies, but you don't have to tell him that). Just show him the door.

After he's vanished, put on your favorite music and dance for at least ten minutes to get rid of any anger that may be energizing your body (which could cause you to lose sleep—was I right or was I wrong?). Then curl up on the couch with a cosy blanket for comfort, play your favorite video and eat up that ice cream to reward yourself. Write in your Book of Shadows or diary whenever nasty feelings of regret come back to haunt you. You've done the right thing.

Excuse 4. She genuinely hopes they'll get back together.
If that's the case, he needs to set her straight. If you're not convinced he has, then he must want something she's giving—even if all he's doing is getting off on the longing.

Savvy solution: This is his problem, and if he loves you truly you'll have to let him sort it out.

Magical help: On a waning moon, take two chilli plants, bind them together with five pieces of black cotton, and name them with his and her names. Then, after seven days, cut the first string. After seven more days, cut the second, then the third, and so on. You will find as you cut the last thread that he and his ex move apart, safely and amicably, forever.

Excuse 5. He genuinely hopes they'll get back together some day.
If he is writhing with unresolved feelings, a lack of closure or whatever, let him finish it. He will want you and her at the same time, but you will get hurt and so will she, and he will probably view the wreckage of his own making down the track, too. So skip the emotional beat-up, and get out of that boy's love town.

Make your own way, with someone who wants you and isn't hung up on the past.

Savvy solution: Wish him well. You might find yourself in his situation one day.

Magical help: Sleep in a circle of sea salt, sprinkled widdershins around your bed, for seven nights. This will cleanse you of painful feelings, refresh your spirit so you can start anew, and prevent you from going back.

Excuse 6. He's confused . . .

Well, golly, see number five. Everyone's as confused as they want to be. Just remember it's up to him to get straight in the head, and you can't help him out there. My advice is to say bye-bye.

Savvy solution: Make tracks and leave him for dust.

Magical help: If you find leaving him a truly heartbreaking thing, take a lily and gaze at the moon. Offer up any angst to the moon, and her light will draw some of the pain away. Truly, she will. She's a tidal workhorse and loves dealing with water, so if you're full of tears she'll work her magic and pull those tears out, so you can move on. The moon never gives you a hard time, either. Later, pop your lily in a vase. When it's shrivelled, and as it dies, your pain will die, too. When you are ready to let go, bury the lily and, as you do, symbolically bury the withered pain of your grief.

Excuse 7. She's a psycho.

Think Lara Flynn Boyle's character in *Wayne's World* or Glenn Close in *Fatal Attraction*. Don't laugh, it happens. Stalking isn't actually a gender-specific activity, just a terribly rude invasion of your right to privacy and a negation of your free will. If it's about love gone wrong and she's got things to say, he needs to help her (within reason) and even maybe go to counselling. Again, within reason. If it's just a serious case of the won't-let-go's, you both need to protect yourselves, and her, from any crazy ideas that may spring into her troubled head.

Savvy solution: Stay safe. Let people know where you are. If she gets dangerous, call the police. Get serious—stalkers can hurt people.

Magical help: Envisage yourself protected by a solidly etheric, white light—kind of like eggwhite—around you. Imagine that all bad intentions and negative actions bounce right off your protective white light. Wear a white scarf around your throat to remind you of this psychic protection. Carry a tiger's eye stone. Draw in your mind's eye a protective star or shield over your property, loved ones and your animals (why do stalkers always go for the pets?).

Try this positive affirmation:

"I now know that my lover's ex is in his past—forever. I am his present, and may wish to choose to be his future. She is over. She is gone. I wish her well in her new life."

However, if he is merely close to a really nice girl he used to go out with, you may need to learn to trust him. Have a little faith, and try this spell to help.

I believe you're true spell

Trust is a major issue and it's your relationship's foundation. It's the unglamorous devils of doubt that can sow the seeds of mistrust and wreck your love nest. Banish them with this.

Find two stones that somehow symbolize the two of you.
Then, with a nail, carve your initials into them.
Then tie them firmly together,
With golden twine (this can be purchased from a good fabric shop or haberdashers).
Keep them under your bed for seven nights,
And make passionate love every night.

Then, bury the stones.
He will never, ever leave you after that week.

If, at any stage, for any reason, you wish to break this spell, dig the stones up and fling them into moving water.

Believe in your beautiful self spell

To believe in your own worth you need to banish all negative energy. You can do this by making a magical smudge stick.

Take a sprig of rosemary,
And a sprig of oregano,
A sprig of basil,
And a sprig of sage.
Bind them together at one end
With red,
Orange,
And sky-blue thread.
Then light the smudge stick to raise your energy,
Banish self-doubt,
And affirm
Your unshakeable belief
In how sexy, lovable and attractive you are.
Say three times:
"I was born beloved,
I will die beloved,
My light shines bright,
He seeks my delight."

Attract your soul mate spell

If you're ready for this spell, get ready for an unpredictable outcome. Your soul mate may have a girlfriend. He may have a more than ex. A soul mate believes in the impossible you, the absolute essence of you—so you're not going to be able to cruise through this one. He's smart, he knows who you can be, and it's his job to get you there. He'll wake you, shake you, pick you up and carry you through the door of self-love, making you crave his kisses. Yum!

Find one picture you love of yourself,
One picture that represents your soul mate
(It does not have to be a person you know—you can try Brad Pitt if you wish—it's whoever represents your ideal man that counts),
One gold piece of paper,
One mirror,
One mauve pen,
One crimson candle.
Gaze into the mirror and chant three times:
"My body moves gladly,
I sing its praise.
My spirit upholds me,
I bless it.
My mind is creative,
I respect it.
My heart warm,
I love it.
I love myself,
As I am alive.
And exactly as I should be.

Blessed Be."
Then write the chant above
Three times on gold paper,
With the mauve pen.
Do this by the light of the crimson candle.
Then paste your picture on one side of the gold paper.
On the other side of the gold paper,
Write down everything you wish for in a soul mate.
Then stick your soul mate picture underneath, alongside, or
even over the list.

When you create this soul mate spellpaper, you're sending a powerful wish list off to the Universal Soul Mate Shopping Center. You *will* get your man—it's destiny, now.

At-a-glance magic for dealing with the ex:

Affirmation: "It is safe for me to be in love. I trust my feelings."

Day of the week: Saturday, for letting go of the past.

Color: Softest green, which actually banishes jealousy.

Stone: Ocean pebble, for firm resolve and gentle change.

Drink: A glass of water mixed with the juice of one lime.

Goddess: Vivian, the lady of the lake, for honesty and wisdom.

Essential oil: Palmarosa, to reduce tension and to smell divine.

Herb: Clover, for luck and for true intimacy with your man.

12

How to say I love you (Without sounding like Céline Dion)

12

Oh my goddess. You've got this far. Big congratulations, and don't forget to tell all your girlfriends how you did it. You're sleeping with each other, waking up with each other, kissing first thing in the morning, and doing plenty of the long stare-in-the-eye stuff (and how good is that!). Intoxicating, isn't it? And let's say that, ooh, at least about five weeks have passed, and maybe there's some kind of tension building up—yep, it's the "Am I in love yet, and when do we start to say 'I love you,'" scenario. Now, some people throw the old "I love you," around like they're some cheap greeting card. Others wait until their deathbeds to give their loved ones some satisfaction. Some people have got some very weird ideas about saying I love you.

No one ever feels "I love you" at maximum intensity, 100 percent of the time. It ebbs and flows, and that's just how it should be, or else we'd all be floppy loveballs drooping around, unable to get on with anything.

It's probably quite likely too that you've been getting into something of a relationship-maybe groove. The Wednesday contact, the establishment of seeing each other on the weekend, the regular sex gig. When it starts building up into not so quality hanging out time, it's a sign that you really know each other. It's all about him being able to handle you watching *Sex and the City*, and you not minding that he plays basketball with the boys sometimes (and comes back for sweaty sex after winning).

It's this groove thing that gives you the space to see what you're both like— and it's the love thing that allows you to handle each other's weird habits. Which is why it's when you're over the "honeymoon" phase of your relationship you'll know if there's love, or if it's been a fling, a practice run, an encore, or an out of season show to iron out the kinks.

Is this intuition (or is this a panic attack?) charm

If something about your new relationship is bugging you, and you don't know whether you've really got something to fret about or if you're just stressing, try this charm for clarity.

Take one piece of blue or white cloth, and stitch it together with golden cotton to form a pouch. Hold it in your right hand, and insert one quartz crystal, four cloves of garlic, four gold coins, sea salt, and one pinch of earth. Visualize what's bothering you. Suspend the pouch in a symbolic place for seven days. After seven days, the thoughts and feelings that linger are the ones you need to pay attention to.

New romantics spell

True romance takes you back to who you really are: you're a mythical soul, on a romantic adventure. There is a sacred power here—romance is legendary for good reason. This spell will help you get in the right frame of mind to confess your love.

On a Friday,
At seven at night,
Anoint two red candles with jasmine and rose essential oils.
Surround each with jasmine, rose, sweetpea or gardenia petals,
And place them at least three yards apart.
Light the candles,

Move back,
Stare into their flames.
Breathe in deeply seven times
And see their flames burning in your own heart.
Every night thereafter,
Move the candles closer,
Until, on the seventh night,
You finally let them both burn out.
Bury the wax and the petals together in the earth,
And know that a new romance is coming to you soon.

Magical powers spell

So, is this it? Is this really going to work out? Or is this another romantic practice run? This spell will help you to reconnect with your magical self. Not only will you know more about your powerful, new emotions, you'll be a whole lot more psychic and sexually enchanting as a result.

Wear silver,
Keep a loving pet,
Grow plants that flower,
Drink dew at dawn,
Light a purple candle,
Color breathe amethyst.
Then, on a Sunday,
Go to your magical space and say:
"Sight for my mind,
Knowledge for my heart,
Strange treasures unwind,

Let my visions start."
Ring a silver bell three times to bind the spell.

Let me be real spell

Who are you? This spell will help you to live authentically, without separation from your dreams, fantasies, desires, flaws, and fabulousness. That way, when you say "I love you," you'll really mean it.

At the dark of the moon,
Prepare yourself a miniature banquet.
Enlighten your room with lemon-colored candles (for cheerful honesty),
And place them on a table covered in pure white cloth (for more honesty).
Pour yourself a glass of wine spiced with herbs (to celebrate who you are).
Include a pinch of these herbs in your feast:
Star anise (for luck),
Basil (for focus),
And rosemary (to remember who you really are).
Eat your banquet, tasting every tiny morsel,
And know that as you eat and drink,
You are returning to the best of who you really are.
After you've feasted, say three times:
"I know I am loved,
For being simply who I am,
And who I am is loved indeed."

Should I stay or should I go? spell

Falling in love is scary. To know if you should keep falling deeper in love, say three times:

> *"I am strong,*
> *I am resilient,*
> *I am capable,*
> *I will honor my true self*
> *with the right love decision."*

Keep an amber stone in your pocket while you are contemplating what you're going to do.

Sleep with amber beneath your pillow, and you will dream of the best possible answer.

At-a-glance magic for saying "I love you."

Affirmation: "It is easy and safe to say I love you.'"

Day of the week: Tuesday—for binding agreements ("I love you, too").

Stone: Moonstone, for protecting rocky emotions.

Drink: Peach nectar, for sweetness and strength.

Goddess: Diana, Goddess of the Hunt (no, not because he's your prey, but for courage).

Essential oil: Rosewood—for long-lasting love.

Herb: Apple, symbol of Aphrodite.

13

Meet the parents (And live to moan about it)

*I*n a world where so many relationship rules have changed, there is one thing that has stayed the same. This applies to you whether you're straight, gay, bisexual, or in a cosmic non-physical relationship—eventually, you get to visit the strange land where he comes from. You get to greet his roots, and they, ahem, get to meet you. That's right girls, it's time to meet the parents . . .

In the past, when you met his parents, there was a reason for it all—you were being presented formally as a prospect to join the family. You probably hadn't slept with him yet. But these days, unless you're a committed fundamentalist Christian (and there's nothing wrong with that—it's just unlikely you'd be reading this book if you were), you've probably swapped bodily fluids, said some pretty racy things to each other, and seen the insides of each other's undies. So dads are a bit weird—they know you've been delighting their son with sex acts they haven't even read about since their wife confiscated that Harold Robbins book in 1976. Moms are a little uncomfortable too—they think you might be stealing their son, the one man who's never let them down.

Now, if they are nice to you, good. Perfect. But if they're not . . .

Danger signs
- Casual mentions of ex-girlfriends;
- Picture shows or slides including ex-girlfriends; or
- Calling you by the names of his ex-girlfriends.

Positive signs
- Asking how you met;
- Asking about you and letting you talk;
- Asking how long you've been seeing each other;
- Complimenting you; and
- Remembering your name.

And just plain scary stuff
- Him handing over a bag of laundry to his mom (or dad);
- Mom wondering why *you* don't do his washing; and
- Discoveries of his children (it has been known to happen).

Cheer-me-up day spell

Every day you need a lift, especially if you're having meet-the-parents hassles. So do this when you feel a little blue or lonesome.

First thing in the morning,
Wear orange to lift your spirits.
Spend five minutes in the sunshine,
And breathe the color blue
For a seven-minute mood-changing meditation.
Dab just a touch of lavender, orange and rosemary essential oils on your pulse points.
And, this is the most important part of the spell,
Plant a fast-growing, cheery-colored, flowering plant (you can plant it anywhere, as long as it is in a place that is special to you).

At the beginning and end of your cheer-up day, turn your face to the sky, stretch out your arms, and embrace life. Feel the bliss . . .

To bind the uplifting effect of this spell, spray some pure water laced with seven drops of bergamot, throughout your bedroom. You'll feel refreshed, be able to tolerate and understand differences, and deal with difficulties with renewed wisdom.

Make them love you, too, spell

Invite his family over, and make them coleslaw with loads of pretty purple cabbage. Purple cabbage blesses unions, so they may begin to see things more your way after tasting your delicious (secretly magical) recipe.

Peel away my anger spell

If that still doesn't work, maybe the best you can do is to release the frustration you may feel in their presence. (This applies to your family, too, by the way.)

Get yourself an onion, and in a dim room, slowly peel away the layers. Have a good sob over the state of things. By the time you have finished you'll feel cleansed, as the onion will have soaked up all your worries.

Next, bury the onion layers in the backyard. Don't let your feelings ruin your relationship—she's only his mom, he's only his dad, after all.

Cool down charm

And if they're really bugging you, you can freeze them. If you just want some time out, write their names on a piece of paper, and pop it up the back of the freezer. This will not hurt anyone or cause them any harm, but it will mean that your paths won't cross for at least one moon.

However, if you're serious about this guy, you're going to have to learn how to get along with his family, at least part of the time.

Hey, love's grand, but it's never perfect.

At-a-glance magic for dealing with the out-laws

Affirmation: "It is okay not to love those whom my lover loves. He respects and loves me more for having my own feelings. I create my own life, and am free to make my own choices."

Day of the week: Sunday (that's when you generally have to deal with them).

Colors: Blue, lilac and silver.

Stone: Pearl—wear them, and they'll be softened.

Drink: Orange, ginger, and carrot juice—their bodies will love you for it.

Goddesses: St. Joan of Arc, Annie Lennox, Xena, and Kwan Yin.

Essential oil: Lavender—wear it and they'll become gentle and loving.

Herb: Lemon verbena, for harmonizing a tense atmosphere.

14

Your place, or mine? (Contemplating the dilemmas of life-swapping)

Not too soon into the whole love affair you may find you just cannot bear to be parted. Oh my goddess, what an understatement. Any magic girl worth her high heels is intense when she falls in love. And my, how you *long* for them, their smell, their funny T-shirts, their body, their everything. And when they aren't with you, you moon about—literally.

Wanting to be with a lover all the time is kind of animalistic—it's about imprinting. You feel wonderful, blissful when you're with each other; torn, separated and anxious when alone. This is the feverish time known as new love, and it's powerful stuff.

Then you do everything possible to spend as much time as you can together, and when you pack your bag for the fifth week, romantic notions of struggling forward in life together, finally a team and not some solo flight into an unknown destination, make the little blinking thought cross your addled mind: Why don't we move in together?

There are tons of good reasons to do this. Why play at it when you can have the real thing? But this is actually a very important decision, so be careful. What do I mean? I mean that if you move in, and it's too soon, several things may happen. You'll get to know each other too soon. You'll fall out of lust, and you'll take a good look at each other and flee, leaving behind a cat, some takeout, and three pieces of unconstructed Ikea furniture in your love wake.

Or, you could learn to like each other, too, and it will be very nice. And if that happens, you could experience what I, courtesy of that goddess of communication, Oprah, call the "works for Doug" syndrome.

Doug and his girl had been living with each other for about three years. They had talked about marriage—like, she wanted to, and so did he, at some stage in his life . . . maybe even with her. But the thing was, he already had everything he felt he needed at that point—they shared money, she washed his clothes, they had sex on tap and the security that comes with saying "Hi" to each other every morning and "'Night" to each other every evening as they drifted off to sleep. Why would he want to get married? After all, the situation as it was definitely "worked for Doug."

Don't audition for marriage by moving in with someone. If marriage doesn't mean much to you, fine. But some people seriously want the whole deal and spend their living-together time in a state of suspended emotional animation, hanging for the day when the question gets popped. Yawn-er-ama. Much better to get things like this out in the open.

Then there are the financial arrangements—sure it's cheaper living together, but how is he with finances? What if he's dreadful at paying the rent, irresponsible with bills and so on. Assess these things with as clear a head as possible, before you move in together.

But, if you do . . .

Happy house hunting spell

Find a blank-paged book and some pictures that fit your idea of a dream house—it could be bold, pretty, or minimal. Then, stick those pictures in your book. Include details of every element of your dream house—they're all-important. If you want a big verandah, find the right picture and paste it in your dream house book. A great bathroom—go ahead. When you've collected these, you can start looking for the place of your dreams.

Before you start house hunting perform this five-sided star spell. A star is the magical symbol of everything coming together, a kind of completeness in your life. It's really as simple as what goes around comes around—and it works.

While flicking through the real estate pages, draw a five-sided star in your mind's eye. Think about the pictures you've clipped out for your dream house book as you are mentally drawing the star. When the star is complete, seal it with a circle of white energy around it.

Now, if you're shown a house you love, draw again in your mind's eye the five-sided star surrounded by a circle of white light, but this time imagine it on the front and back doors of the house. (You don't actually have to be there when you do this, just visualize the house and send out the energy, if you don't want to be caught looking a bit loopy by the real estate agent.)

Bless this house party ritual

Get together a group of friends who won't be too embarrassed at the neo-pagan turn of events about to take place. Or else you can replace a couple of the items here, to avoid outing yourself as a fully fledged witchipoo.

If you move in together, even though you're not exactly getting hitched, you are making a pretty big commitment, taking a pretty big risk, so you both deserve to be loved and supported by your near and dears.

*Gather plenty of good white wine,
Plenty of yellow candles,
Plenty of spicy ginger fishcakes,
And a kooky quartz crystal.*

Wait till everyone's at the party, and play some cool ambient music. Next, light one of the candles, gather your pals together into a circle and all join hands. Then say:

*"I dedicate these candles to good works, good times and good loving
in this house,
We hope to share our happiness with you, our wonderful friends
and family."*

Then, take the crystal and pass it from person to person (yep, a bit hippy, but everyone will love it). Each person should make a wish for your happiness out loud and proud.

Read a love letter you've written to each other—it can be as personal, funny, loving, or soppy as you wish—it's totally up to you. Then exchange presents—jewelry is extra good for this. Antique earrings, a watch to keep track of your time together—whatever, as long as it's personal. Then pass around the yummy cakes and eat them. Drink a glass of the wine and raise a glass in a special toast to your home and happiness.

Pack a little gift bag for friends—a beautiful house ornament would be best. Then you'll get the benefit of all those kind thoughts. What a great way to start out together.

If things are going well, get together again on the same day once a year and reaffirm your love for each other.

No money hassles spell (or, The art of tree reading)

This one's a simple, pretty, and very, very fun spell. Get yourself three green ribbons; one to represent money, one for growth and prosperity, and the other for fresh energy. Lots of length in those ribbons now, because you're going to be stringing them high up a tree.

Now, head out to the garden, or the nearest potted plant, or even a tree you like in a nearby park. Choose a tree or any plant (one that you just love the look of and feel some kind of connection with). Think about your hopes and ambitions for the future before making your decision. Maybe you'd like to choose a tree that seems to symbolize your dreams. Are you going for a great new job or a change of career?

Try a tree a couple of years old. You can choose frangipani for its flowering sweetness—just watch that no branches get snapped off (it can be a little fragile depending on the season). You can choose an avocado tree for all of its fruit, blossoms, and its flexible limbs that can deal with high wind, periods without water, and are way tougher than they look. Or choose a magnolia, for its rare burst of beauty. The personality of the flower or tree will blend with your money and love personality. Like everything that's natural, trees can be unpredictable, so keep watching out for great reading opportunities, like new growth, abundance, and sudden spurts of leaves or flowers.

Next, tie the three ribbons on a branch that has plenty of new growth coming out of it. Don't tie the ribbons in front of the new growth—you need to get behind the energy, you see, so you have to tie your ribbons behind the new growth. Focus on sending positive energy to the tree and affirm to the Universe that as it grows, so will you prosper.

The way the tree itself grows from now on will symbolize the prophesy for you, and changes or patterns coming up in your life. For instance, three new limbs can spring out of a branch, symbolizing diversity in your working life. As long as they're healthy and growing, that's fine. One career path may, in time, take precedence over the others—you'll know that's the case when one limb begins to be longer and healthier, or blooms with more flowers, for example. This would indicate that you'll ultimately move toward one direction.

When the ribbons are way taller than they were when you first tied them to the tree, and when their color has faded with time and weather, you're going to be in a much better financial situation than you are right now. It will then be time to cast the spell again, to acknowledge the new phase you are entering.

If you want to cast this spell for prosperity as a couple, entwine two green ribbons tightly together and tie them to your symbolic tree or, better yet, plant your own tree, which you both nurture and read together.

Love shack magical gardening

Out the front of your house, plant a gardenia and a magnolia.

Out in the back yard of your house, or in a sunny back room in pots, plant a strong, fast-growing climber, such as jasmine, or a fragrant bush like lavender.

Good herbs to plant about the house, in a window box if you can, include:

- St. John's wort—this will banish depression and ill-will;
- Pennyroyal—replaces anxiety with harmony;
- Lemon verbena—brings peace within your home from the inside; and
- Lavender—promotes peace from others.

If you have any hassles with neighbors—and who hasn't—plant something pretty and spiky (a climbing rose is good) between the borders of your home and theirs.

Other plants that look soft but are actually tough little nasty-energy averters include bougainvillea and bird of paradise. And for really tough neighbors, try planting some flowering cacti between you to end their troublesome ways. If they get too horrid, try scattering kitty litter at their back door. Then they're sure to leave you alone—especially if pussy cat helps you out and thoughtfully pees on it.

A magic charm for an in-love home

Into a pretty little bottle, put some rose petals, lavender leaves, feverfew, rose quartz, and a single strand of his hair and yours tied together with red thread.

A tiny pinch or fragment of each of the magical ingredients is fine. Don't go mad trying to squish an entire rose bush and a giant slab of quartz into a wine bottle—it won't make your spell any more powerful. It's your love energy and willpower that make it magical.

Keep the ingredients little, simple, and symbolically very, very powerful.

Charge your spell with love energy by holding the bottle in your left hand, near your heart, and thinking about everything you wish for from love.

Seal the bottle and bury it with love and optimism near your front door, saying three times:

"I enter my love, my luck and my hopes into the very heart of this house. I bless our house,

I bless our love,
I bless our life."

If there's no way you can dig up under the front door, that's okay—try the front garden, or a window box in the front room. Don't tell *anyone* about it. This spell will secure your happiness and your future together—if the Universe deems this is your true destiny. Remember, if things change, that is for the good of everyone involved—including you.

At-a-glance magic for living together

Affirmation: "I am free and loyal in love. I choose to share."

Day of the week: Sunday, for celebrating togetherness

Color: Butterscotch—a blend of hues with beautiful results.

Stone: Opal, as its contrasts make it beautiful and unique.

Drink: Green tea—drink it to energize your choices together.

Goddess: Juno, so you can be a wise queen in your new castle.

Essential oil: Tangerine, to spice up your love nest for as long as you wish.

Herbs: Fennel, celardine and cedarwood

15

When he thinks your taste is suspect (Or, when smart lovers have silly fights)

He can't believe it. He can't understand how this has happened to him. He had everything sorted, he knew exactly what he was doing with his life. He just can't believe it. (Excuse me, I hear you say, what exactly is it that he can't believe?) He can't believe he's going out, maybe even in love with, a woman who:

- Likes Britney Spears;
- Wears loads of make-up;
- Has a different point of view from him;
- Asks him not to get drunk every time they're out;
- Drinks Coca-Cola;
- Talks to plants; and
- Reads self-help books.

He is astounded at himself. Apparently, he sees his tolerance of your horrible habit as a kind of flaw in his perfection, that somehow (you witch, you) you've cast a spell on him and he can overlook your taste crimes in order to be with you.

Most sensible guys don't care about this sort of thing. They know you're you, that he's him, and they don't care that you love Oprah, read *Bridget Jones's Diary* or delve into books like this. It's a chick thing and he knows it.

He, on the other hand, may love things you do not. So what? It's called accepting personal boundaries. Personal boundaries are where you accept you're you and he's him. You don't need 100 percent agreement. Nor do you need to criticize him for what he likes.

Some people need to merge, to be accepted by their lover the same way they'd be accepted by, well, a dog or a stuffed toy. If your beloved is the kind of man who bosses around other people's children or puppy dogs, he just may have a little bit of a control issue—and you may, once the love daze slowly lifts, be affected by that.

Ladies and gentleman, not accepting differences that are reasonable is a major problem in matters of love and harmony everywhere. Remember, you are not an extension of anyone else. Nor is anyone an extension of you. When you love, your beloved will not always agree with you. When you are in love, it is possible to have an argument, or just accept the differences between you both. You can be different, and still live long and prosper together.

So, how to magically solve silly arguments? Try this mystical hoodoo for getting together without worrying about being the same person. In voodoo tradition, a mystical marriage helps the man and woman get together and love each other truly, madly, deeply. Each of you must devote an entire day to the other—yep, that's right. Whatever he wants, you do it. When it's your turn, the opposite applies. However, the day means no sexual activity. It's all about listening, giving presents, cooking food, taking each other out, and making each other happy. Why no sex? Because, too often, we use sex to solve emotional problems, and that can lead to resentment.

The love hassle over stupid things charm

One of a magic girl's most important accessories, apart from her spellbinding personality and her intuitive way of applying the perfect shade of red lipstick, is her tarot deck.

Open the magic circle:
Take your deck of tarot cards and shuffle them as you reflect on the issues that are giving you grief.
Divide the deck into three with your left hand.
Then join them together again in whatever order you feel is right (again, with your left hand).
Next, draw three cards and place them on your left side, upon some red cloth.

Draw another three cards and place them in the center of the red cloth. Draw three more cards from the deck and place them to the right of you, again on the red cloth.

The **cards on the left** represent the underlying issues of the past that are creating this situation—it could be conditioning, parents, previous love disasters or other hassles, like work, career, or health.

The **center cards** represent the way of the heart—what you are experiencing emotionally in the present—and offer some clarity regarding what's actually going on with you two. Why are you fighting over ridiculous things? The middle path will help clarify the real reasons for you.

The **cards on the right** will offer you some indications of what's going to happen as a result of the combination of your history and your present dilemma.

After you've interpreted this spread and made some notes in your Book of Shadows, take a further three cards from the pack. These will indicate the way to go from here—exactly what action to take.

If you wish, you can devote this ritual to Aphrodite, as you may want to receive her energy and guidance. While you are within the magic circle, concentrate particularly on the outcome card, the very last card you draw, which you lay out above the three on the right. Really investigate its imagery for clues.

Just in case things at home are a little heated, you should probably clear the air with a bit of space-cleansing before settling down to do this ritual. So, before you begin, burn some rosewood or jasmine oil.

Throughout this ritual, burn a blue candle to uplift you, and to help you think clearly. After you have closed the magic circle, burn the red candle to say thank you to Aphrodite. Place a lily in a vase, (just a single flower) where you'll be able to see it from time to time—this is your reminder to view events with some perspective.

Friday, Aphrodite's day, is definitely the best day for this kind of seeing into your future—I bet you're already making a blissful one.

At-a-glance magic for banishing love boxing matches

Affirmation: "I can get away with fighting—what I don't want to get away with is being an unhappy person."

Days of the week: Saturday—for ending quarrels, and Wednesday—for communication.

Color: Softest baby blue, for peace and serenity.

Stones: Rose quartz and ruby.

Drink: Make each other a chamomile tea with manuka honey.

Goddess: Aphrodite.

Essential oils: Lavender, rose, hyacinth and hibiscus.

Herb: Dandelion, to detox your love relationship.

16

You don't bring me flowers
(Or, baby, where did our love go?)

So, you're in love. You're together. And it's great, isn't it. *Isn't it?*

Oh, so it's been a while since those all-night sex sessions were interrupted by catnaps and struggles to tear yourself away from him to go to work (job, schmob). And those flowers he *used* to appear at the door with—now, that was nice, wasn't it?

If it's been a while since you and your beloved had the glimmer of a hot moment (let alone a hot date), you may be suffering from post-honeymoon syndrome. He may be ranting comfortably now, no longer worried if he offends you with his tirade against Oprah Winfrey. He knows you love him—so should you, he's been telling you you're a goddess for about four months now. He's exhausted by all this adoration. He needs to relax.

Top 10 reasons for a love slump:
1. You've slept with each other for more than six weeks;
2. You know he's your steady date on a Friday night;
3. He says "Hi, it's me," instead of "Hello, is that you?";
4. You're happy all the time. (Amazing how fast the cocoon can get a little snug);
5. There's been a big TV event—such as *Big Brother*, a *Sex and the City* marathon, the *Superbowl*;
6. Your parents or his parents have been to stay with you for three weeks;
7. Something really bad has happened at work and you feel very flat.
8. Exam tension;
9. You're broke; or
10. He's broke.

The end result is, you can't help thinking sometimes that this falling in love thing isn't quite the payoff the gigantic lust-fest at the beginning led you to believe it would be.

If you're lamenting the loss of the man in hot pursuit, and getting just a little tired of how all he seems to want to do now is fall asleep in front of the TV at 8:00 p.m., don't despair! It's not too late to revive that love action again. All it takes is a little magic.

But be sure you do this occasionally. Even though it's good to get on with your lives, there's always room for a gigantic love revival.

Here's the magical touch you need . . .

Love Revival spell

Inspiration can sometimes be as evasive as the money for those Manolos you've been drooling over. This sexy witchcraft spell is going to restore your sex symbol energy, and you're going to feel utterly connected to an unlimited source of electric vitality, humor, and cha-cha-cha energy. And Persephone is just the deity to call on when recreating yourself in the image of a sex goddess:

On a Tuesday night, during a waning moon,
Cleanse your bedroom of all unsexy clutter.
Then, light a white candle in your refreshed boudoir within a circle of sea salt.
Now you have cleared and cleansed your space,
Stand naked before a mirror. Perfume your pulse points, and Call on Persephone three times.
Feel the sexual energy reignite your desire.

Fascinating contradictions spell

This spell will awaken the paradox inside you, and allow you to express who you can really be in the world—full of contradiction and, thus, fascination. Think Marilyn Monroe fretting over the meaning of Dostoevsky, Nicole Kidman reading Pushkin, Cleopatra bathing in asses' milk, a librarian in Agent Provocateur stockings, and your mother swooning over Brad Pitt . . .

Use the magical power of pink light if you're short on loving feelings,
Blue light if your moods are swinging,
Green light if there's no money for one perfect coffee to start every day with,
Yellow light if you're feeling cold toward others and can actually pass a homeless kitten without reacting.
Breathe in your preferred hue of magical light from the Universal well of beauty, innocence and radiance.

Practice this until it becomes natural, and true creativity will flow.

Fire, fire burning bright—future forecast spell

As you think about where this relationship is going, here's a handy spell—especially if it's cold and there's a fireplace in the house.

This spell has its origins in the Middle Ages, when witchy girls would huddle by the fire and use the flames of the yule log to divine the future.

Say three times:

> *"Fire red and burning well,*
> *Into your depths I cast this spell,*
> *Knowing that where I now dwell,*
> *My future soon to me you'll tell."*

Then poke the fire once, twice, three times. Notice the sparks that fly up the chimney after you finish poking the fire.

Fast, plentiful spits and sizzle mean a hectic start to the new spring, with heaps to do and barely enough time to do it in.

Several loud pops mean shocks to your current way of life, so be prepared for change. If one of the pops is very loud, there could be a new and very powerful love interest in the spring.

Slow burning hisses mean you'll have time on your own to contemplate what's been happening in your life, and where you want to go.

Pop a toasty sweater on, and put out the fire safely.

The following spell is extra special as no-one knows you're doing it—it can all be done in your head . . .

True romance body lotion

Make this magical body lotion to get those loving feelings stirred up again. This potion will attract your lover, and he'll act like he's just seen you for the first time across a crowded room—and all he wants is you.

Take the petals from seven red roses and place them in a mortar. Lovingly drizzle a small amount of sweet almond oil over them, and slowly grind with the pestle. Focus all your loving thoughts, desires and all your sensual feelings on this process, and charge the potion with your own powerful magic.

When you've ground the petals and almond oil into a smooth paste, add seven parts of sorbolene for each part of the mixture, and blend.

Store your potion in a colored glass bottle to shield it from sunlight (the sun's rays will rob your potion of its strength). After bathing each night, stand naked before your mirror and slowly smooth the potion over your entire body.

Repeat seven times:

"I love and honor the beauty and workings of my goddess-given body,
And I thank the Universe for its health and the pleasure it brings
to me,
And the joy it brings to my lover."

Enjoy the sensual feelings provoked by this powerful love potion, and breathe in its scent.

This is a simple spell, but it's very powerful and can have strong results. For maximum power, repeat this once a week for seven weeks, commencing on a Friday night (for Aphrodite, goddess of love, beauty, and all tender feelings).

At-a-glance spell guide for vagabond hearts

Affirmation: "It's better to stay and play than to run away from a relationship. I embrace change, and revive my inner sex kitten."

Day of the week: Friday (you're going to be busy!).

Color: Scarlet will revive ardor.

Stone: Ruby.

Drink: Absinthe—it's decadent, romantic, and delicious.

Goddesses: Isis and Daphne.

Essential oils: Jasmine and heliotrope.

Herb: Catnip will re-excite you both (just grow it—never eat or drink it!).

17

Relationship ambiguity, modern girl and guy style (Or, don't you want me, baby?)

17

*R*elationship ambiguity—it can strike at any time. It can be a feeling of love ennui—that French word for the flat feeling that we all encounter from time to time. No joie de vivre (those crazy French people have all the good words!).

This is the stage where we can look over at our loved one after waking up and instead of gazing at him, thrilling quietly over the way the shadow of his eyelashes fans the edge of his sharp cheekbones just so, we see . . . a man. Just a guy. With imperfections. Maybe he's even snoring.

If you're piqued about the deal you think you've got here, you'll focus on the snore. Then you'll start obsessing over little things, like how he doesn't brush his teeth as thoroughly as you do. What's he so relaxed about? you wonder. Why isn't he a little more eager to please? He's so in his comfort zone. And you're pissed off about it. And you're saying to yourself, "Is that all there is?"

There is an explanation behind all this. Most of us modern girls were reared with very un-modern stories that had some guy, usually a prince, or a wannabe prince, straining after somebody he wanted so badly he felt he had to throw everything but the pursuit of her away. It's intense. It's romantic. It's completely unlikely. And, if your romance started out that way, be warned. It's completely unsustainable. (That's why so many hot affairs can't stand the reality of monogamy. The friction, the secrecy gave the lovers their heat, not the desire to love.)

Good looks and great smells are completely out of reach first thing in the morning, unless you want to live in a state of constant panic. Panic leads to insecurity, and both are very bad. It's just not healthy for magic girls to leap up and apply make-up after, say, six weeks of loving.

And so, just as some men (and women) think women need to look perfect all the time in order to be worthy of love, some men don't meet *our* expectations either. So, what to do.

A little time-out may be called for. Under no circumstances abandon the relationship—that's simply buying into the whole push-them-away-so-you-can-win-them-back pattern that some people make a virtual career out of.

What to do . . . There's spellcasting, of course. Magic really can show you what's going on behind those troublesome romantic myths. But don't give up empathy (a very magical girl quality). You see, he may be going through similar things himself. Hasn't he seen you flossing? Perhaps he, too, is seeing other women moving in languorous, dangerous slow motion down the street.

What to do? You know, even though it seems daunting, this love dilemma's not too hard.

Magical affirmation:

"I allow myself the honor of mulling over my feelings. I allow myself the freedom to wonder what the future is, and to ask the hard questions. It is always safe to ask questions."

Light-hearted laughter spell

Humor, giggling, cracking up, laughing at his jokes (never at him—no matter how much you want to). Laughter and light-heartedness is a truly under-rated magical quality. There is so much to be delighted with in your boyfriend that this will help you see the light. Besides, laughter is endearing, sexy, and boosts your endorphin levels.

*Every morning for a week,
Squeeze the juice of one orange
(for sustaining love),
Cut up one banana (for healthy thoughts),
And five strawberries (for lust and romance).
Throw all of the above into a blender.
Whiz away, then drink immediately, while you chant:
"Happy happy,
Joy joy,*

*I really love
My boy, boy."
Or something equally as silly and
feel-good.*

Fill your oil burner with the essential oils of grapefruit, lime, orange or bergamot all day long to enhance the magical power of light-heartedness.

Does he still love me apple spell

Here's a really simple, idiot-proof spell for lovers with a touch of the yeah, it's you again, I can see that.

Just take an apple (a really yummy one—that's the hardest part of this spell) and slice it in two. Give one half to your partner, and munch on it together. Say "I love you" while doing this.

If he replies "ditto" or just grunts assent, he loves you too—passionately.

Spell to reawaken his love

This will re-ignite your love interest, and you too.

Let your hair fall free, pop on a scarlet slip-dress, go barefoot and gloss those lips. Use perfume. Now:

*On a full-moon Friday,
After seven at night,
Close your eyes
And breathe in delight.*

Whisper your name
And call your beloved.
Do this for seven nights,
He'll be re-discovered.

Say his name three times while arranging seven dark red roses in a crystal vase filled with spring water, and adding seven drops of rose oil.

For the hour after the spell (the binding hour), burn some rose oil and feel the power of true love speeding through your blood again.

To seal the spell, eat a bowl of strawberries, knowing that every seed on every strawberry carries the seed of true love's return to your heart. To top it off, watch a sex goddess film like: *Some Like it Hot*, *The Seven Year Itch*, *Gentlemen Prefer Blondes*, or *The Misfits*. If you can't find any of these, any film starring Vivien Leigh, Hedy Lamarr or Brigitte Bardot will do.

Put some empowering, sexy music on. Try Debbie Harry, early Madonna or PJ Harvey. Ahh. You're very replenished now. You're his Venus—go tell him what's your desire.

At-a-glance magic for deciding your relationship's future!

Affirmation: "I allow myself the freedom to choose. I trust myself."

Day of the week: Saturday, for endings and new beginnings.

Color: Green, for soothing nerves and seeing the future.

Stone: Bloodstone, to know what's in your heart.

Drink: Chai tea, for spice and serenity.

Goddess: Actually, let's ask for the help of the angel Gabriel on this one—he will intervene and improve the situation.

Essential oil: Basil—not sexy, but excellent for thinking clearly.

Herb: Lemon, to help you to distinguish between good and bad.

18

Mating calls
(That strange phase when he—or even she—flirts with others)

People flirt for all sorts of reasons. These include:

- It is fun;
- It is natural;
- It reaffirms your sexual attractiveness;
- It makes you feel powerful; and
- It makes you feel sexy.

Stop right there! Check out those last three items on the list. What's going on when you flirt to make you feel *those* things—could it be the bad personality specter of power games have raised their head in your love affair? Maybe you thought a little love testing was due on the agenda? Oh dear.

Now listen. When you love someone, you oughtta flirt with *them*—yep, that's right, the one you've already got. But sometimes when the slide into ugh-booted comfort happens, one of the victims in its path (apart from your impeccable standards of personal hygiene and new clothes for every date) is your self-esteem.

And when that first flush of heat cools, you can relax—and what a relief that is. But sometimes you can miss that feeling of being utterly desirable, absolutely wanted, right here, right now, no, I can't wait, got to have you . . . You know what I mean, don't you? Okay. I mean, it should be just fine for you to relax into the relationship, right? Isn't that exactly what you've been after? And for anyone, you *or* him, trying to maintain ultimate ardor 100 percent of your time together is just plain . . . exhausting.

So you settle in. But what happens? Instead of being stoked at this little turn-off upon life's love path, you're vaguely pissed off. Where are my flowers? And what do people do? When they get a bit too relaxed, they flirt with other people. So instead of each other, this couple, in love but bemused at where the heat's gone, simmer with the others at parties. Now, that really gets their attention, doesn't it? And I bet the sex is good when you finally get home, too—even if it is a little bit angry, and you're still not sure what it all means the next day.

Mating Calls

I have some girlfriends—smart, creative girls, too—and they hate it when they feel their gorgeousness is being neglected. So when they and the beloved head to a social gathering, they go mental, practically pole dancing to try and get as many phone numbers as they can. Then they fling them at the (bemused, jealous, cranky, horny) beloved's feet, triumphant, as if to say "See, I am attractive." (Of course you are—you were pole dancing, but the less said about that the better.)

Sure, flirting means acting out being single. Yes, it means setting up a promise that's probably going straight down the road to nowhere—but hey, anyone can feel when they're not wanted 100 percent of the time, even if it's only gone down to about 75 percent.

Lift up those emotions secret soak
(Or, how to keep a cool head and a very warm heart)

Happy vibes will result from using this potion in a bath every Monday (and maybe for seven days, depending on how you're behaving and feeling).

Run yourself a lovely warm bath on a Wednesday night—Wednesday is the day of communication, and working on this aspect will help you get over any love paranoia you may be experiencing. Add jasmine (for love), basil (for clear thinking), and sandalwood (for protection).

Soak for as long as you like. When you're finished, you'll see that all fear about being dumped or cheated on, and all your doubts about other women being more attractive to him than you are—the general volume of the blah blah blah of your frightened heart—drain away with the water down the plughole.

First thing every Monday, Wednesday and Friday, meditate on where you want to go in your life—this is about learning to love you and your own life more. Burn a blue candle for clarity and clear thinking.

Exercise hard at least three times a week, when you're scared about relationship issues or other chicks stealing your man. This will burn away the anxiety, banish paranoia and give you heaps of endorphins so you feel happy. If worse comes to worst, just remember to be yourself and to run your own life—and be happy, and loved, because you are beautiful—really. Don't stop believing that.

Go-go glamour spell

Why do we need glamour? Because when our man flirts with another, it dents our self-belief in our inner sex goddess. When she is wounded, we feel like a be-cardiganned grandma—even if we are wearing Norma Kamali. When we embrace true glamour, it empowers us (sorry to use a very seventies word, but it does).

Glamour is a kind of image we project, and its essence affects the world. It is about being charismatic, larger than life, memorable. It doesn't mean you have to laugh madly or have a cigarette holder and furs—you can be a quiet person with plenty of mystique, too.

Witches of the past, present and future use glamour for confidence, for disguise, for spying, and for confusing the enemy. You can even use glamour for camouflage: think Nicole Kidman with crimson lips, wearing vintage Halston fresh after her divorce . . .

Warning: You can only pull off glamour when you are brave enough to connect with your inner Academy Award-winning goddess. But once you get in sync with her, you'll be a flame to which men are drawn like moths, against their will. Be prepared!

Wear crimson red on a waxing moon of a Monday,
Seven dabs of your favorite perfume (on the inside of both wrists, above
and below your navel, on the back of each thigh and one on your crown).

Halve a perfect red apple,
Sprinkle cinnamon on top,
Eat half at dawn,
The other at midnight.
And as you eat, know that your inner charisma is rising to the surface,
And shining for all to see.
Now go out there and shine like the star you are, you gorgeous thing!

If you can handle its power, you can do this spell on a big night. Just be sure to carry your apple somewhere unobtrusive.

Now, flirt with him and see if he ever wants another girl again. I think not . . .

At-a-glance magic for being flirty

Affirmation: "I am a witty, pretty woman."

Day of the week: Wednesday, for arranging dates and clever conversation.

Color: Turquoise or silver, for sexy mermaid overtones.

Stone: Topaz, for courage in dealing with new people.

Drink: Pernod, as it's flirty, but unusual. Plus, it won't be possible to get too tipsy, so you'll stay enchanting and safe.

Goddess: Psyche, for understanding what the sexy subtext to that witty repartee is.

Essential oil: Patchouli—just the sweetest little dab, mind you.

Herb: Mint, as it will make your breath simply delicious.

19

The pointing of the toilet lid
(And a thousand other domestic conundrums)

*Y*ou've said the L-word, you're hanging, and you still think he's adorable, then suddenly a huge love god monkey wrench is thrown in this work in progress called "Magic Boy and Magic Girl get together." It's when he starts getting relaxed and way too casual i.e., the toilet thing. You know. He goes in there, uses the last scrap of paper, and won't change the roll—what's with that anyway? Apparently, the boy manual says he has to lift the lid so he doesn't soil the seat (nice touch), but then he has to leave it up. Why? We don't know why, and this isn't the place to go into the evolutionary advantages of leaving details like this to the womenfolk. One thing's for sure, it's annoying. It makes us feel like we're the world's relationship cleaners. And it makes guys look scarily old-fashioned.

Some other housekeeping sins may include:

- Gradually undressing throughout the house, celebrating his manly nudeness, without actually returning the said clothes to their appropriate enclaves;
- Leaving many pairs of shoes under the coffee table;
- Not folding the laundry. Instead, standing looking confused at clothes in the machine before turning away, defeated;
- Leaving ugly-looking things in places clearly intended for beautiful girly displays;
- Forgetting to take out the recycling—particularly sinful, as he has probably been the biggest contributor to the amazing array of beer bottles;
- Being unable to cook without creating a chef-like disaster area, and forgetting that the only kitchen hand available is you;
- Leaving used lengths of dental floss on the coffee table before your parents come around; and
- Putting clothes that you have washed on the end of the bed, getting into bed, and kicking the clothes off onto the floor. Then putting them back onto the dirty laundry pile, complaining of having no clothes to wear.

Domestic bliss? Hmmmm.

Restore my bliss spell

Combine in a spritzer ten drops of lemon verbena essential oil, one rose quartz stone and as much pure spring water as you need to fill the bottle to the brim.

Shake till it's as fizzy as you feel.
Madly spray the potion in areas of most aggravation,
On a Saturday.
Your stretched nerves will be resprung by the time the bottle is emptied.

Calm me down before I break up with him spell

This one is simple.

Starting on a Saturday,
Eat a red apple,
And do so each night for the following six days.
Chew over the problem as you crunch the flesh.
Pull out the seeds from the core,
And call them his housekeeping sins.
Then dispose of them between the time the sun sets and the first star is visible.

Sunrises and sunsets are extremely powerful natural magic. You can work all sorts of spells just by focusing and watching the sun rise (for what you want more of) and set (for what you wish to kiss goodbye).

What if these spells don't work? There are millions more potential boyfriends out there for you, and with each one comes variations on the theme of domestic dilemmas. Most boys are just not good at picking up after themselves (what else is the floor for?), washing your clothes (do not let them try, unless you fancy a shrunken Donna Karan sweater, or your perfect white shirt from J. Crew be-pinkified), or doing any of those other domestic duties. Don't give up! Maybe some of these domestic spells will do the trick.

Boyfriend training spell

Feng shui experts say that an open toilet lid is akin to throwing money out the window of your car when driving very fast through a major shopping center. If he's the slightest bit superstitious, or keen on money, he might start to close the lid if you tell him the risks.

If he does begin to respond, reward him . . . Positive feedback makes for pleasurable long-term changes in behavior. Show him who's a domestic goddess by training him to treat you right.

Celebrate being a domestic goddess ritual

Wearing a flimsy negligee,
Chanel #5 (or any perfume with a jasmine base),
A suggestive smile,
And no bra.
Steep in red wine,
Mulled over soft heat,
Herbs of your choice.

Drink from a ceremonial goblet,
And toast to your victory,
With every sip.
See yourself emerging
Into a gorgeous home,
Victorious,
Joyful,
Sexy.
And know that it is safe to win this love battle,
For there are no losers,
Only more sex,
True love,
Less mess,
And a cleaner toilet to gain . . .

At-a-glance magic for domestic bliss

Affirmation: "Change is a Universal truth."

Day of the week: Saturday, a day of endings (and of cleaning).

Color: Lilac, for persuasion, and blue, for resolve.

Stone: Granite, because it's tough and beautiful. You will endure!

Drink: Cold beer—for both of you (hops will calm you down, too).

Goddesses: Martha Stewart, Grace from "Will and Grace," Nigella Lawson, and Oprah Winfrey.

Essential oil: Tea tree oil will de-stress you, and it's good for cleansing.

Herb: Choose the Bach Flower remedy Rock rose, to alleviate the panic attack you will have when you see the toilet seat up (again).

20

PMS for boys
(Or, why the female of the species is deadlier than the male about six days a month)

So. For about a week before your period, due to hormones ebbing and shifting, you can, if you're sensitive to these sort of things, er, kind of lose it.

Do I mean women are insane for a week? No, no, no. But you may, if you have to handle the lurking demon that is PMS, find your patience strangely thin, your tendency to get angry high and wide, your ability to feel critical, picky, bloated and, sometimes, um, bitchy, surging forward like a tidal wave. So, welcome to the fertile years of womanhood.

Now, we know this will pass, and there are ways to handle those days, and if people were just sensitive it would all work out okay. But the thing is, it's hard for men to get it—at all. How can they, given we've only just let the lid off the secret? Our mothers never even used to admit they had periods, so now that we do, we need to let men know how to live with us while we're having them.

When we have PMS-inspired tantrums, all practical attempts at having a nice chat about hormones fall away and have to be taken up on another less pre-menstrual day. So, to reconcile themselves to their scary new part-time girlfriend, guys comfort themselves with thoughts like "it's just a moment of temporary insanity."

It doesn't have to be this way. PMS, or the time when you're feeling all riled up, can be a fantastic time. Really. If you take the power surge analogy, think about how angry and powerful you feel when you have PMS. Now think what you could do with that energy, if you just channelled it in a positive direction.

I always save writing letters of complaint to banks, gigantic airline companies who've taken away all my frequent flyer points, and ranting at the general state of the world and maybe even doing something about it for when I have PMS. Whatever deserves to be at the end of your power, whatever needs changing—and I don't mean your partner not matching pillowcases and sheets—use that outrage to turn a hose on injustice, fire off a brilliant e-mail, or ring your accountant and ask when your tax return is arriving. Because you have PMS, you won't be intimidated, and you'll demand fair play. Being nice won't get a listen to, which is fantastic.

However, this fired-up, change-the-world-in-five-minutes fervor may tend to make other citizens of the world, like your boyfriend, jumpy. So don't rant at him—use your energy where it will show. Exercise. It will relieve the desire to practice karate on your dividing walls, get endorphins pumping and release the need for that gigantic stress cry. It will also soothe away symptoms like bloating, cramps and fatigue when your period does make its appearance (signaling a retreat into niceness, usually). Make sure you eat well. Include essential fatty acids to balance the hormonal swings by eating tuna, salmon, nuts, and seeds.

Don't listen to crazy doctors who like to put women on medication to bland us all into serene Stepford Wives. Having PMS when used right (for good not evil), can be a powerful and constructive thing. Your period is not your enemy—and PMS can be positive, if you can learn to work with its intense energy.

Write away your PMS

Your Book of Shadows can also be used as a diary—it's your friend and your lesson book, and it should be used as a tool to record the ups and downs of your particular individual menstrual cycle. You can also use it to record your spells and rituals, and the results you get. It's where you can ponder and dream. Where you can ask questions, even if you don't have any answers. Every witch needs a Book of Shadows, even if it's just to release some annoyance or grievance at the man in her life, especially when she's suffering PMS.

Try dividing your book into thematic sections based on moon cycles, times of the year, even your menstrual cycle (though that does seem a bit hippy). Just record your thoughts in it as often as you can and you'll find that the symptoms of PMS settle down. This is because you'll be able to gradually peel back the layers of your life and see the cause and effect of problems, enabling you to treat them at the root and not at a symptomatic level. Which is very witchy, and magical, indeed.

Back to earth spell

When the moon is either waxing or full, head outside under the magic of its most powerful rays. Find an old tree, and stand beneath its spreading branches. Take off your shoes, and really plant your feet into the earth. Visualize the strength of the planet beneath you, its energy pouring upwards through the soles of your bare feet.

Raise your hands to the stars, and really thrust them skywards. This will release any negative energy or stress that your physical and etheric bodies may be holding on to. Breathe deeply into your belly for about one minute, and feel your levels of personal strength increasing.

Once you have finished this, lower your hands and head home safely.

Grounding crazy energy spell

On a Monday, under a waxing or full moon,
Plant your bare feet in the earth at sunrise.
And do this again at the last chance you get at night.
This will draw some of the powerful spikes of energy away from you,
And ground them in the safety of Mother Earth,
Thus increasing your levels of power,
Without harming you with your own tendency to surge through the day.

Quick fix for harried boyfriends

The best way to make your boyfriend feel special, after you've had a hormonal rant, is to cook a romantic meal for you both.

Place a whole, free-range chicken in a baking tray and lace it with 40 (yes—40!) cloves of garlic. (If you are vegetarian, use a giant pumpkin instead of the chicken.)

Before you begin to bake, carve the rune Ansuz into the chicken (it looks like a capital F, with the top line slanted to the right like \). Ansuz is the rune of intellect, inspiration, and great communication. Its power comes from the Norse god Odin, who was the god of poets and all inspiration. Simmer in the oven in a shallow pool of red wine for two hours, or until cooked.

Next, add a yam or sweet potato to the menu. Then carve the rune Sowilo, which represents the sun and its path, into the vegetable (this looks like a lightning bolt). The yam or sweet potato represents femininity (that's you) and the rune represents clarity, strength, and the power of the mind.

This magical meal will renew your energy, refresh your thinking, and heal your wounded feelings, if there are any lurking around.

Exercise, witchy style

PMS, or hormonal mood swings, star fits, and regressive tantrums can be balanced out by exercise—the only hitch is that it needs to be kind of regular. Three times a week for 20 minutes will make a difference. Exercise releases things called endorphins, neurotransmitters found in the brain that make you feel happy and positive. In fact, that's why people get hooked on exercise—they can't give up the euphoric feeling that the endorphins give them.

You don't have to go mad, though. Here's a workout designed to handle your menstrual moods—and maybe save your relationship (grateful boyfriends can send me flowers).

Exercise one: Heart-to-heart

You need to get plenty of cardio exercise, so walk or run gently for 20 minutes each day. The deal is to raise your heart rate long enough for your whole system—and all those pesky internal organs—to benefit.

Exercise two: Routine matters

Get down on all fours and breathe in and out gently but deeply. When you're ready, on the out breath, pull your tummy up towards your spine—kind of try and suck your belly button through to the other side. This will work your abdominals, and ease cramps.

Exercise three: Be a biker girl

Lie on your back with your head raised and your arms by your side. Try to stay as relaxed as possible. Raise one leg and slowly extend it, then return it to the first position and do the same thing with your other leg, a little bit like you're peddling a bicycle.

Exercise four: Back extension

This is a great one. Lie on your back with your arms relaxed yet straight by your side. Place your feet on the back of a chair and feel the stretch right through your back and spine. Keep your ankles, knees, and hips in one straight line and your head, neck, and shoulders on the floor throughout this stretch.

Exercise five: Do the pelvic thrust

Lie on your back with your feet on the ground and knees bent. Place your hands against the small of your back and tilt your pelvis back. Your aim is to flatten your back hard against your hands. Stay there for three seconds and then release and relax.

Do the workout above three days a week and watch you body improve and your mood swings retreat. You'll simply feel energized—not like a cranky, scary girlfriend.

Moody girl blues busters

Eat plenty of foods with vitamin B—wholegrain breads, basically. The impatience and irritability which you experience days before your period are due to a drop in phyto-estrogens. Be sure to eat plenty of soy-rich products as they will help balance the battle going on in your body as those levels plummet. You can also take an evening primrose supplement, which has tons of essential fatty acids as well as the added benefit of making your skin really luscious, plump, and smooth. For an alternative source eat loads of tuna, salmon, and nuts such as almonds.

Problem: Water retention.

Magical solution: No wonder you're in such a bad mood—if someone pricked you with a pin, you'd water the garden. Water retention is a real pain, and to ease it you need to reduce your sodium intake—ideally you should keep it to between 920 mg and 2300 mg a day. Check labels to see how much salt packaged or tinned foods contain. Increase your fiber intake with plenty of raw fruits and veggies, which will keep you feeling less like an enormous water-retaining dam.

Problem: Muscle cramps.

Magical solution: Magnesium is your true friend. It's a mineral that eases muscle cramps, and makes you calm and relaxed. Magnesium supplements are available from your pharmacy. Tofu is also said to be good for anyone who suffers nasty cramps.

Problem: Junk food cravings.

Magical solution: All I want to do in the days before my period is work my way, like a woman possessed by the junk food demon, through mountains of gorgeous dark chocolate. Cravings for junk food like mine (these cravings can be salty or sweet, by the way) are about comfort, and evening out your mood. Try to eat more fruits, breads, and fish instead, to get the same satisfaction. Again, vitamin B can ease those cravings, while it balances your moods.

Problem: Fatigue.

Magical solution: If you're completely wasted in the days before and during your period, have your iron levels checked. Eat red meat, spinach, and maybe take a B6 supplement. Regular exercise will also combat the overwhelming urge to lie down. Never binge exercise as it doesn't do your body any good and it sets you up for failure.

At-a-glance magic for PMS damage limitation

Affirmation: "This, too, shall pass."

Day of the week: The chances are that every day is going to be a bad day, so forget it.

Colors: Black, red and deepest purple.

Stone: Not while you're feeling like this. The less you have to throw, the better.

Drink: Warm milk and manuka honey.

Goddesses: Hecate, goddess of the underworld, Shakti the destroyer, and Elizabeth Taylor in "Who's Afraid of Virginia Woolf."

Essential oils: Rose geranium and lashings of lavender.

Herb: Chamomile, to soothe your frizzy nerves.

21

How to mend a hurting heart (Or, how to have a good break-up)

Ouch, so *that* romance certainly didn't work out. You know, that *should* be okay—it's not going to be magical with everyone you test-drive. So why do you feel like something deep within you crumbled? It could be that you just really, really want to fall in love, and see life as a bleak, Siberian-steppes-type place without a man around.

You know, when it comes to relationships, I don't think there are any of the following mythological men out there:

- Other halves—you don't need someone else to make you whole. You're whole as long as you're striving to reach your own potential, and you're a whole lot more attractive when you're doing that anyway; or
- Perfect matches—no-one, repeat no-one is perfect. Brad Pitt likes to fart in bed. George Clooney cannot commit. David Beckham is not Albert Einstein. You can't get everything you need from the one person—but you might get a great love affair going if you just accept them for the best they can be, if you know what I mean.

Believing in these mythological men leaves you feeling incomplete—like something's missing. And of course that's how you're going to feel. But the thing is, if you're wandering around like a member of the walking wounded tribe, you're not going to get happy easily—it would be an insult to your tribal brothers and sisters. The bottom line? You'll be devastated every time the latest date just doesn't feel right.

When you're really witchy and confident, you should be able to work your way through a veritable NFL defensive line of men without feeling you have to intensely love and wrenchingly leave everyone you share a skim cappuccino and movie with. Be inspired by Jerry Seinfeld, sleeping nearly every week with a different girl, following his nose into endless romantic (okay, maybe just girlfriend-type) encounters, and saying at the end of every single episode "see ya," with no visible pain. Why? No, not because it's a prime time TV comedy. Because he had three people he liked, sort of, to hang out with and workshop his love life with.

You don't have to be quite as shallow as Jerry—remember the episode where he started to feel and couldn't handle it?—but you can take a leaf out of his fat, little black book. You don't have to get dramatic about everyone you break up with. You need to just move on if it just doesn't seem like it's going anywhere. And no, it doesn't matter if you've slept with him.

Don't do that thing where you convince yourself you have to stay because:

- You've had sex;
- He likes you;
- You've been looking for a while;
- You're desperate; or
- You're practicing.

However, you can stay involved if:

- No-one's going to get hurt (who are you kidding—someone nearly always gets hurt, so let's revise this to: make sure it only hurts a little bit);
- The sex is great and you need the exercise;
- He makes you laugh, and you're not stressing about finding love;
- You're just enjoying the moments; or
- You could do with some male company, and it's not too heavy on either party's side. (Let's face it, you could meet a mate through your new pal).

Once you stop hanging your love hat on every man you meet, date, or sleep with, you'll realize the world is a bigger and better place than you may have been giving it credit for. You will find someone great for you, you don't have to settle. Go, hmm, hmm, hmm, nyahhhh, maybe.

You know the diligence with which you shop for a perfect pair of summer sandals? Or the ultimate dress for that cocktail party? The scrutiny you subject lipstick shades and textures to? Start using your intuitive discriminatory skills on the men in your life, too.

The courage to get out there and amongst it spell

It's no good working on love stories in your life if you don't leave the house after one bad date. You've got to be strong. So here are some ways to begin to feel truly excited about mixing it with other two-legged talking creatures again and again and again.

There's nothing like the fear of walking into a party—it's a great test of courage, in its purest form. Never be fooled. Parties can be joyful get-togethers, but they are all human zoos where competition and pecking orders can be established and maintained, making them altogether terrifying.

So if you do feel freaked at the idea of a room full of strangers, remember that everyone's frightened of being judged. That's why people get excited about parties—they're like a performance. What we project can be a concentrated aspect of a part of our whole personality.

The trick is to know we are frightened, but to act as our inner party girl instructs.

Inside each of us is a heroine, a goddess, an inner wisdom that can help us put fear aside and walk unscathed through whatever situation it is we are frightened of. Even if it's a big party.

During a Tuesday of a waxing moon,
Wear something gold to signify your courage shining . . .
Anoint a yellow candle with neroli, tangerine, or orange oil,
To sustain your courage,
And to light up the darkness
Where fears hide and thrive.
Connect with your own heroine
By asking her three times to give you strength,
To make you bold,

Make sparkling conversations,
Dance like a wild thing,
And attract lots of attention.

So, are you over it? spell

Ready to move on from that let-down man? Not really, but willing to give it a go? Good for you.

On a Saturday night, when the moon is waning,
Draw a soft, warm bath
Into which you have scattered three handfuls of pure rock or sea salt.
Then gently place one free-range egg
Into your tub.
Light an indigo candle
And bathe in its light.
Rewind the tape of all your sad love stories,
And allow any feelings that may arise
To come to the surface.
Any lingering pessimism, bitterness, anger, hurt, or sadness
To stream out of your feet,
Through the water and into the egg . . .
When you pull the plug on that bath,
You will literally feel the pain of the past drain from your own body and mind.
Then, just to be on the safe side, take your egg outside,
Under the soft light of the waning moon.
Bury it at least six inches deep in the earth.
Sprinkle some water mixed with a few torn verbena leaves.

Now you can move on with your new life.

The "I feel much better now that I've done this spell" spell

You'll feel much more glued together after this if you're a bit upset. No more hand-wringing Maria Callas impersonations. (Or is that just me?)

In your bedroom,
Place a long white candle.
Rub the candle with bergamot for protection,
And lavender, to soothe your emotions and calm your spirit.
With a handful of sea salt,
Make a circle around your bed,
In a counter-clockwise direction.
Light the candle,
Just before you go to bed.
Read an inspiring book, or gaze at beautiful images.
Then leave it lit,
While you sleep deeply.
When you wake up,
You'll feel renewed, refreshed,
And ready to live and love again.

At-a-glance magic for breaking up (without breaking down)

Affirmation: "This is what it is. I can deal with it. I am never alone."

Day of the week: Tuesday—for dealing with problems with courage.

Stone: Lapiz lazuli, for healing, protection and perspective.

Color: Aquamarine, to uplift your spirits.

Drink: Jasmine tea, to promote self love. Avoid alcohol.

Goddesses: Hecate—for wisdom and independence, Jerry Hall, for glamour in moving on.

Essential oil: Sandalwood, for acceptance and healing.

Herb: Ginger, for cleansing the past and coping with the present.

22
The Ultimate Chapter

When is he supposed to propose? (And so on)

*T*his is the big one. A little flashback to set the scene. It used to be that once you'd been together between six months (at least) and about twelve months (and that was pushing it), you'd announce your intention, to your families and to the world, of staying together for at least this lifetime or, oh well, till the divorce fairy came.

Fast forward to today . . . Now there are so many choices regarding relationships, it's hard to know whether what you want (the sparkly rock, the big white veil, the meringue gown to make your mother howl with happiness) is valid. Or if being married is actually worth it. Or whether you're a free spirit who doesn't want to get married but really really wants a white wedding dress anyway.

Whether or not the world keeps changing and the divorce rate keeps climbing, even if your parents rocked your world by announcing their intention to divorce, most girls I know still have a special time-keeping mechanism deep down, or maybe not so deep down, in their heart—they want to get married. They want to be loved deeply, and symbolically. And it's not all about the ring, or the gown, or the princess tiara from Tiffany's—well, maybe it is, a bit . . .

We want a beloved man to say loud and proud in front of everyone we care about, "I love you, and will love you, for the rest of my earthly days. I'm one lucky man." We bask in that kind of stuff. And realistically there's probably only one chance at having it, and that's our wedding day. I mean, he's not likely to say it over sausages at the next cookout you go to, is he? Oh, he is? Well, hang on to him!

So, when is he supposed to propose?

I still think the old rule of thumb mentioned is worth applying to your situation, no matter how modern you may be. Not that it has to be that way—you know, getting married à la the traditional time span. I do know people who have been together for four years before he finally squeezed the question out.

But does it really take four or five years of living together, or constantly being with each other, to know you want to give it a go?

I say no, because marriage is, above all, a leap of faith. It's a pledge, not a guarantee, so it's bound to have its challenges. You can't rule out desire's ups and downs, but if you stay together you'll regularly fall back in love and into lust with your husband, and that's the best experience of all. And the life you have together can be wondrous, because it's got history *and* a future. You won't have to keep revisiting your old self with new partners and the endless repetition of the cycle of dating. You can move on with your life, and love someone.

Goodness, I came over almost evangelical and pro-marriage there, but what can I say. I'm a convert. So go into it right—like, getting along, feeling magical and good with him—and you'll probably continue that way, unless there's some major personality flaw that you didn't subject to my wise and highly suggested magical testing. Then you'll know better next time, anyway.

But then there are people who rush into it. If you want it too fast, it could be you've got some notion of the ideal love thing, and he's just the latest contender for the part. If you've been together for about six months and you're still in love and you're around 18, why not hang in there and see what happens. I'm a bit of the mind that waiting a little is simply smart thinking. If you're really serious about the life-long thing, why not start saving together so that when you do say "I do" you'll be one of those exceptional couples who, by the grand old age of 27, has saved enough to travel beautifully and pay off a fair bit of their first home.

If you're heading towards 30 (okay, hurtling), then you may be thinking after six months, especially if he's around the same age, that things are looking good for a lifetime together. And if you're happy, really happy, and you're working through instead of around any problems, you're right. So I reckon if you haven't heard any peeps out of him on the subject by the time you've been seriously dating for about one year, you have to start making inquiries. Embarrassing? Don't fool yourself. Much more embarrassing to suppose that what he wants is you, forever, when he may just be treading water, or have no intention of asking you. Do you even know if he wants to get married at all? If the answer is no, then you're definitely overdue for some question time.

Let's get together spell

Write your name and that of your beloved on a red red candle. Anoint it with rose oil and light it on a Friday. Burn it for seven minutes, and for each subsequent night until it burns down to the wick. Then either bury the wax in the earth, or fling it into the ocean or another natural source of water. (I know this sounds like I'm all for polluting, so if it bothers you, as it does me, you can use beeswax, as it's natural and will break down.)

Within one moon, you and your beloved will discuss the topic of marriage. You can take it from there.

Knowing spell

Tune into your intuition simply by paying close and soft attention to your breathing for five minutes every morning. Always do this at the same time and in the same place so that it becomes a daily routine to teach you how to be still and calm. Even if you're not in your special room or place, carry something from there to evoke the centering effect the meditative state has—it could be incense, oil, a petal, or a scrap of luscious silk. In this state you will bypass the you, and go into the soul-merged state. In this state, you will see what is true.

This meditative technique will help you apply big picture feelings and philosophies to love hassles—like the biggest one of all, "Will he marry me?", so you'll be able to see from a distance what will happen.

Love-frustration cure

Color breathing is a meditation technique that achieves quick emotional results. Visualize breathing in the color pink and you will feel soothed, loved, and loveable.

Breathe this color in deeply, and exhale a lighter pink. See the loving pink energy enter your body and run through your veins, reaching into every cell, empowering you, and emanating from your pores as a kind of love glow. See yourself beaming at your partner, who is smiling back at you. Reach out your hand towards him and see him reaching back. Walk towards him and open your arms for the embrace. Feel the wonder of holding your beloved as he enters your arms.

Through the air drift magical streamers of turquoise blue, silver, pink, and gold. Make the streamers circle you both until they intertwine their vibrant colors, which are alive with beauty, the air singing with their movement. Slowly they gently wrap around you both, pushing you closer together and binding you as one force against anything life may bring. You are dressed in a veil, with flowers in your hair, which is free and beautiful. You wear a gown of the palest lilac, with a green and white border.

He wears clothes of bronze and green. Nature's own garland wraps around his strong legs. Slowly, the ties that bind you dissolve into your flesh, becoming part of your being and changing your essences forever, by the handfasting ceremony.

You are together, one spirit, and are fated to be so until you break this spell (this can be achieved by visualizing your bindings being unwoven with the same ritualistic intensity). Until that time, which may never come, you are joined, and your wishes and blessings can become yours, with the power of the Universe and its all Loving spirit.

To keep true love alive...

Burn rose oil,
Bathe in jasmine oil,
Remember lilies can bring love when brought into the house on a full moon.
Rub down your dry skin with oil and salt, to purify and renew yourself.
Recreate your love with imagination and erotic sensuality.
Respect your love's mystery.

Obtain a beautifully aromatic blend of coffee beans (if you drink it), which contain the magical flavor of vanilla. Vanilla is made from orchid seed—decadent, erotic, and irresistible. The vanilla will keep your love so alive, you'll keep this coffee close by. Don't overdo its magic though. Grind the coffee beans, and as you do, say three times:

"Magic bean of delight,
Bring (name) and I together in passion tonight."

Your love life won't look back. It's no mistake that coffee gives you energy, so have a cup late afternoon, for early evening loving.

Make love at different times

Don't just make love after a big night out or in the morning; make love during the day, while the sunlight energizes your bare flesh. Make love together in a safe place outside

Be alive to love and to sensuality. The rewards are richer than anything material. This transformation is what we live for.

Bless your union by respecting it,
Keep it alive by nourishing it,
Let it be banal at times, and love that.
Revel in its security and adore familiarity for its comfort and ease.
Find beauty in the ordinary
Then celebrate with ravishment,
And delight in your senses and the myriad worlds of your love.

Remember, l'amour is beautiful, it is team work, it is struggle, it is sensuality, it is well worth wanting and even more worth living for. Love is tender, kind, and good, and there is not enough of it in this cruel world we have made and need to magically heal.

Love loving and never be ashamed of romance. Be wary however, of projecting your dreams where they do not belong. Love where love will grow, and you will have given and received the greatest of all gifts in this life.

Marry me (or I'll lose my mind) spell

This is a fresh take on a traditional marriage spell, and it's a good one.

To enchant a ring for marriage,
Buy one of common metal
Plain and narrow, colored gold,
To fit your wedding finger well.
Drop it in a vessel filled half with wine, half with water.
Add one oak leaf, one of willow,

Two of bay and one of grass.
And the name of the one you wish to wed,
Written on silver paper.
Keep the vessel covered tight
Near a window,
In the sun
From crescent moon until the full.
Then rub the ring and wear it hidden
On a string around your neck,
But never tell the name you seek
Until you take it for your own . . .

(. . . and if you don't want to take his name, well, that's okay—it's the desire, the drama and the commitment of this spell that counts.)

Meanings of precious stones

So, you've completed your spells, and the relationship's in full bloom. Why not make yourself familiar with some essential knowledge for women in love . . .

Diamonds

Diamonds are supposed to be forever. They signify a kind of purity of your love, that will last a long long time. They are also extremely precious, and are great investments. These days they are more ethically mined—thank goodness.

Rubies

These are nature's passion stones. Rubies connect you emotionally and sexually and are pretty intense, so go for a wild ride if you dare. They are precious, and rare.

Aquamarine

These are often given as reminders of personal symbols. Tom Cruise gave Nicole Kidman a *lot* of jewellery when they were together, and one of his gifts to her was a pair of diamond and aquamarine earrings. Check out her eyes and you'll see why. They are very beautiful stones, and signify praise of your personal qualities, your spirit and your individuality.

Emeralds

Emeralds signify that you are precious and rare, that your beauty is eternal, and as natural as the green of the trees around you, and the green of the sea as the sky darkens at night. They are the stone of Venus.

Topaz

Topaz is all about sensuality—the lush curve of your thigh, the awkward length of your arms, the way your hands move just so. They can also be about your eyes—hazel eyes have the same golden hue as topaz, and reflect kindness, caring and soulfulness. Topaz, while sensual, is also a spirit stone.

Sapphires

Twinkle, twinkle, little star. Sapphires are the celebrities of the stone world, and they signify that you will always have first place on the stage of your lover's life.

Pink diamonds

Pink diamonds express the ultimate in femininity, you minx, you. They imply a certain mystery and flirtatiousness—an ultra-girly girl, if you like. You have a sassy approach to the relationship, and he loves it that way, so don't go changing.

At-a-glance magic for making it forever

Affirmation: "True love can last forever, and I am truly in love."

Day of the week: Sunday, for asking another to be yours forever.

Color: White, for the rebirth of yourself in love.

Stone: Diamond—your love will never wear out.

Drink: Champagne, to toast your future! Congratulations, you're in love, together, and looking towards a happy future.

Goddess: Aphrodite, the queen of lovers, is on your side.

Essential oil: Rose—the purest, rarest form. Splash out!

Herb: Valerian, for the peace it brings in the midst of excitement.

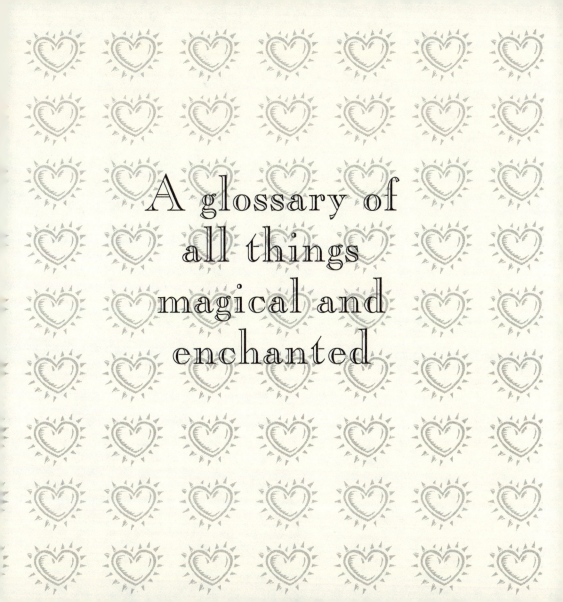

A glossary of all things magical and enchanted

Affirmation: Affirmations are powerful little mottos or sayings that you carve into your consciousness through repetition. What you think becomes who you are. Affirmations can help you achieve almost anything.

Alchemy: When one thing becomes another. Traditionally, this was the dark ages and medieval science of converting one element into another. You can use alchemy just by boiling water!

Altar: This is the sacred workbench in your sacred space. Treat it with loving care, and all sorts of good things will come back to you.

Amulet: A charm or piece of jewelry traditionally used to protect the wearer against evil. These days, amulets are worn to give extra power when spell-casting. You can make your own amulets out of anything that you wish. For example, a traditional locket, filled with rosemary, becomes a strong reminder of personal love and power. How you use it is up to you.

Aspect: This refers to the magical truth that gods and goddesses (like humans—think about it) have many faces, truths, or identities. You could focus on an aspect of a goddess: for example, Minerva's wisdom, in a spell.

Binding: Some kind of symbolic act or verse with which you tie up the loose ends of a spell, to give it a sense of closure and added power. You can literally bind something by stitching up (such as a magical pouch) to complete the spell, binding the dress of a magical doll, or by quoting a verse three times at the end of your spell. "So mote it be," traditionally binds spells. The modern equivalent could be "As I so wish it," or "So it happens."

Cakes and wine: This is an old way of saying share food with others. Whenever you share magical food with others, you get them involved in your magic. All food is magical, anyway, but you must be very careful that this is done in an extremely positive, for-the-good-of-all kinda way—because otherwise the power of three times three can really get you.

Casting: For some enchantresses, gathered sticks, stones, and shells are not just symbolic items for their altar. Some people use these found objects to cast and foretell the future. These can be stones, tarot cards, rune stones, or anything, really—bits of old pizza cartons or leaves from a tree are just as useful. The idea is to collect objects that signify certain things to you—maybe they look like places, symbolize people you know, or embody certain qualities. Then you cast them, and read the future from the pattern in which they fall.

Casting a circle: When some enchantresses work magic, they cast a magical circle around themselves and their sacred working area to protect it from negative influences (or maybe just from the noise of roommates next door!).

Cauldron: This is a magical pot, which you can cook things in. Just use an ordinary pot if you like, or you can make some patterns on one you already have. You could even buy a special one—most Asian supermarkets have great fireproof clay pots which can be used for broiling, steaming, and cooking.

Chanting: Chanting is not something exclusive to Hare Krishnas. As baseball crowds know, if you chant something over and over, you kind of auto-hypnotize, and go into a trance-like state—this is great for making magic. It doesn't do your head in like drugs or alcohol most definitely do, either. It's also very good for your mind and your internal organs.

Charge: If you do invest in any crystals, talismans, or magical tools, charging them means to give them a good blast of your psychic power. This means you identify with them, and they kind of become at once a part of and an extension of you.

 To charge a symbolic object with your own energy, hold it in the palm of your left hand. Next, take your right hand and place it over your left. Feel the energy pulsating between your palms, and visualize this essence entering your object, becoming an invisible yet powerful presence. This energy will protect your special keepsake, and will symbolize who you are and what you want.

Consecration: It sounds scarily like church, but it's not. It means to make something sacred, and to dedicate it to a higher power—it could be the Universe, the sun, the moon, grass, forest, waves, oceans, dolphins, sexy guys—you name it. After the object has been consecrated it will work its magic for you in the name of whatever the higher power was.

Coven: Hmm. I am cautious about covens. Sure, 13 heads can be better than one, but whenever you get lots of people together, you get a lot of ego and competing ambitions—too many politics, too many hidden agendas, too many power struggles. I think it's best to practice discreetly and on your own, certainly at first. Follow your own path, and do good as you know it to be by your conscience.

Now a witchy team of four, I have more patience for. Good friends can help you. Think Willow, Tara, Buffy and Anya. All different, but supportive, with distinct and individual talents.

Divination: Simply the foretelling of future events. You can use anything for this—grains of sand, the petals of a flower, a tarot deck, or the fall of moonbeams. Use your imagination, and ask the Universe. You'll never be told, literally, by a big booming voice, but you'll be sent clues, and they can really help.

Elements: Earth, air, fire, and water; North, South, East, and West. The unchangeable, the eternal. These are energies, without which there is nothing at all . . .

Evocation: Calling something. This can be scary, and usually totally unnecessary. Only call on good stuff. Bad stuff will always hurt you in the end, even if it's just in your own head—the most likely place for it to happen.

Familiar: Generally, an animal or pet which you care for. This is very likely to be a cat or a dog. All pets embody something of the wildness of nature, and even something as simple as growing plants or keeping birds can make you closer to the natural forces of the Universe, and thus you become a bit more magical. Pussy cats are great as they're stealthy and clever. And so are dogs—they're protective, loyal, and have two natures, the doggy friendly one and the wild, wolfish one. You can do worse than using your pampered pets as inspiration.

Fire: The South in the Northern Hemisphere, or the North in the Southern Hermisphere. Fire can also be symbolic of the color red, energy, passion, willpower, love, war, and blood.

Book of Shadows: A book of your own magical spells and charms, or someone else's, from which you learn (or get really confused). Forge your own path for a more magical existence.

Grounding: As described before, you can get your head way out there with enough magical work. Feeling lightheaded and drained is not all that unusual. You have to come back to earth to avoid walking into traffic, talking to spirits at work, or freaking your new boyfriend's parents out at dinner by talking about your visions of dolphins flying through the cosmos. So, grounding thus comes into its own.

Find yourself a good-sized patch of soil or sand outside. If it's in a park, lie under a tree in the shady soily bit, and if you can manage it, take off your shoes and get your feet stuck right into the earth. Breathe in and out *very* slowly right into your belly, for a while. Relax. Feel the energy pouring into you. Say thankyou to the earth. There, you're back, to your worldly, sensible self, ready to do all the ordinary things a girl's gotta do.

Healing: You can help channel healing energy from the earth, nature, the elements, or other good places like the Universe in lots of ways—the idea is that you become the link between the source and the person who needs help. Simply sending them positive, magical thoughts can do people so much good.

Initiation: This used to be when you went through a symbolic and sometimes scary ceremony to welcome you into the world of witchiness. Now, I would advise just doing the sacred searching for yourself, and when the time is right, you'll work out your own little ceremony. There are some simple, spicy suggestions inside this book, so keep it simple, and stay away from so-called witches bearing pentacles and scary knives.

Invocation: When you call upon a god, goddess or a spirit to help make your spell shiny and special.

Karma: This term means that whatever you do will come back to you. In spellcasting, we reckon it comes back three times, so send out good energy rather than negative, in order to reap the rewards. Just a thought—it does not mean that you'll get everything you want, or that everyone will be nice. Rather, what it does control is how you respond to events and people.

Lunar cycle: This is the 28-day magical natural system where the moon visibly waxes from dark to full, and wanes to dark again. Try and work magic with the best possible lunar time for your purpose—so no, no, no hexing around full moon time, I'm afraid, or it'll be a nasty power of three that bites you back.

Meditation: This means emptying out your conscious mind with the help of breathing and mantras or whatever. Meditating helps to slow down your mind and your metabolic rate, and enables you to listen to your higher self—who you are, blood, breath, self, and soul.

Necromancy: Oh dear. This is the thing that happened at slumber parties, remember, only you called it making a ouija board and getting freaky messages from dead people. Please don't muck around with this stuff. Whatever your belief system, it'll do your head in unless you're gifted and protected. You and me, we're beginners in the world of the undead, so please be careful. Don't play with dead people.

Occult: This word means hidden, so when people say they're into the occult, they mean they're into the mysterious or the unknown. The problem with this word is that it's been usurped by people who like reading about serial killers and Aleister Crowley. You can do magic without trailing around in black lace, fishnets, and purple hair, and you don't have to listen exclusively to Marilyn Manson and Sisters of Mercy (not that there's anything wrong with that, it's just that it can be a cliche, and you don't need to be something you're not to be magical).

Pentagram: The pentagram is a five-pointed star, which reflects and symbolizes all phases of life for every living thing. Some people say that if you turn the pentagram upside down it can be used to work black magic and call on the devil. I say, run away, very fast, from those people, and don't believe a word they say.

Planetary days: Every single day is associated with gods and goddesses, planets and transits, and, oh, the list is exhausting. I've given a simple explanation in the introduction, so you can plan around that without feeling like you're sitting a trigonometry exam.

Quarters: The moon has quarters and so do the elementals. Quarters is a snappier way of saying the elements and their associated directions.

Ritual: A ritual is a sacred series of actions that you perform in order to work some sexy magical enchanted stuff. In the end, you meet your goal through positive ritual and actions which strengthen resolve.

Sacred space: Any area you've purified in some way so you can work your magic without obsessing about last night's pizza orgy.

Scrying: This is the ancient practice of gazing into a body of water's surface, unfocusing your eyes slightly, breathing regularly and seeing what visions spring to mind. Just gazing into bodies of water is relaxing and tends to make you day-dreamy anyway, as surfers, fisherpeople, and mermaids know.

Talisman: A talisman is a magical object infused with power—you can give it to someone, use it to work some magic, or empower your own self with its power. For example, if you use a crystal as a talisman, and infuse it with protective power, you can wear it when you are around your boss at work, and you'll feel so much better.

Temple: A grove of trees, a church, the beach—anywhere special to you.

Thaumaturgy: The working of wonders or miracles when you cast a spell to protect yourself on a date, your house, your car, or to keep your mom safe when she goes on a trip.

Uncasting: Unworking a spell, or re-opening your magical circle at the end of a spellcasting.

Visualization: Whatever you visualize just might happen. This is so much more true when you actively "imaginate" things into existence. By visualizing what you want, you're actually rehearsing its existence by preparing the ground for its arrival—so it's a very powerful, easy, and fun magical tool that every girl should use.

Ward: Just like Robin was Batman's ward—only without the homoerotic underpants. Seriously, it's when you agree to be someone's protector, usually if they're going into a psychically or emotionally tricky situation. It's like agreeing to be someone's guardian.

Wicca: Literally means wise, but it's kind of a hippy way of saying witchcraft. It's also more associated with the nature-worshipping activities of magic and spellcasting. If you make magic, you can call yourself a wiccan, if you really want to. Nothing is compulsory, except happy thoughts.

Widdershins: Counterclockwise. Clockwise is called the wacky name of deosil—but, get this, in the southern Hemisphere, counter clockwise *is* deosil. Why? Because the movement of the sun through the sky is counterclockwise.

Zenith: When either you, your spell, the season, or the moon is at its peak, this is referred to as the zenith—or the maximum point of power. A time bursting with psychic mega-wattage, and an amazingly effective time to cast positive magic.

Index

A

Absinthe, 158
Acceptance, of differences, 147–50
Affirmations, 15, 215
    for attracting guys, 54
    for banishing love boxing matches, 150
    for breaking up, 200
    for dealing with ex, 120
    for dealing with his friends, 100
    for dealing with in-laws, 134
    for distinguishing good guys from bad, 62
    for domestic bliss, 181
    for first dates, 70
    for first sexual encounter, 78
    for flirting, 173
    for friends and boyfriend merger, 93
    for good sex, 105, 107
    for living together, 144
    for mood swings, 192
    for proposals, 211
    for relationship's future, 162, 165
    for relationships on the verge, 85
    for saying "I love you," 128
    for single girls, 43
    for vagabond hearts, 158
Alchemy, defined, 215
Alcohol. *See* Drinks
Altars, defined, 215. *See also* Sacred space
Amber, 127
Amethyst, 93
Amulets, defined, 215
Anger, spell to banish, 133
Ansuz, 188
Aphrodisiacs, 105–6
Aphrodite, 4, 70, 107, 128, 149, 150, 211
Apples, 128, 163
Aquamarine, 78, 200, 210
Aquarius, moon in, 36
Arguments, petty, 147–50
Aries, moon in, 35
Aspect, defined, 215
Astrology and spell casting, 35–36
Attracting guys, 47–54
Attracting soul mate spell, 118–19
Authentic self spell, 126

B

Bacall, Lauren, 85
Back extension exercise, 189
Back to earth spell, 187
Bad guys, distinguishing good from, 58–62
Bad sex, 103–7
Banishing doubt spell, 116–17
Basil, 105, 107, 165
Bath, to revive emotions, 170–71
Beach dates, 66
Beauty spells, 68–69, 117, 171–72
Bedrooms, of boys, 73–74
Beer, 106, 181
Bells, Tibetan, 12–13
Beltane, 34
Bergamot, 12, 25, 62, 91, 112
Binding, defined, 215
Black, 78, 192
Bliss restorer spell, 178
Bloodstone, 165
Blue (color), 21, 54, 62, 134, 150, 181
Blues
    cheer-me-up spell for, 132
    solutions to, 190–91
Body lotion, true romance, 156–57
Book of Shadows, 24, 114, 218
    recording dreams in, 31
    recording menstrual cycles in, 186
Boyfriend(s)
    accepting differences, 147–50
    breaking up, 195–200

Boyfriend(s) (cont.)
  ex-girlfriends, 111–20
  first sexual encounter with, 73–78
  his friends and you, 97–100
  living together, 137–44, 177–81
  meeting his parents, 131–34
  proposals, 203–11
  roadblocks to meeting, 39–40
  saying "I love you," 123–28
  training spell for, 179
  your friends and, 89–93
Boys. See Guys
Boys' night out, 97–98
Breaking up, 195–200
Breathing, 205
  color, 15, 206
  fresh air, 18
Brown, 21, 100
Butterscotch, 144

C

Cakes and wine, defined, 215
Calendula, 70
Calming spell, 178–79
Cancer, moon in, 35
Candlemas, 34
Capricorn, moon in, 36
Cardamom, 105
Cards, Tarot, 28, 148–49
Casting, defined, 215–16
Casting a circle, defined, 216
Catnip, 158
Cattrall, Kim, 85
Cauldrons, defined, 216
Cedarwood, 85, 144
Celardine, 144
Cerridwen, 100
Chai tea, 165
Chamomile, 25, 192
Chamomile tea, 150
Champagne, 211
Chanting, defined, 216
Charge, defined, 216
Charm(s)
  in-love home, 142–43
  intuition, 124
  love hassle, 148–49
Cheating, 111–20
Cheer-me-up spell, 132
Chemistry quiz, 104–5

Chemistry tricks, 105–6
Chocolate, 105–6
Cigarettes, 18
Clary sage, 27, 54, 100
Clear-outs, 11–13
Clear quartz crystal, 62
Clover, 120
Cloves, 106
Coleslaw, 132
Color breathing, 15, 206
Colors, 20–21. *See also specific colors*
  for attracting guys, 54
  for banishing love boxing matches, 150
  for breaking up, 200
  for dealing with ex, 120
  for dealing with his friends, 100
  for dealing with in-laws, 134
  for distinguishing good guys from bad, 62
  for domestic bliss, 181
  for first dates, 70
  for first sexual encounter, 78
  for flirting, 173
  for good sex, 107
  for living together, 144
  for mood swings, 192
  for proposals, 211
  for relationship's future, 165
  for relationships on the verge, 85
  for single girls, 43
  for vagabond hearts, 158
Commitment-phobic guys, 61
Consecration, defined, 217
Contradictions spell, 154–55
Cooking spells, 91–92, 132, 188
Cool bad guys, resisting, 60
Cool-down spell, 133
Cosmopolitan (drink), 43
Courage
  essential oil for, 113
  herbs for, 20
Courage to get out there again spell, 197–98
Covens, defined, 217
Crazy energy, spell for grounding, 187

D

Dandelion, 150
Daphne, 158
Dates (dating), 81–85. *See also* First dates
Days of the week, 19–20. *See also specific days of the week*
  for attracting guys, 54

for banishing love boxing matches, 150
for breaking up, 200
for dealing with ex, 120
for dealing with his friends, 100
for dealing with in-laws, 134
for distinguishing good guys from bad, 62
for domestic bliss, 181
for first dates, 70
for first sexual encounter, 78
for flirting, 173
for friends and boyfriend merger, 93
for good sex, 107
for living together, 144
for mood swings, 192
for proposals, 211
for relationship's future, 165
for relationships on the verge, 85
for saying "I love you," 128
for single girls, 43
for vagabond hearts, 158
Days of the year, best for spell casting, 33–35
Demeter, 85
Diamonds, 70, 209, 211
Diana, 4, 62, 128
Differences, acceptance of, 147–50
Dionysus, 106
Divination, defined, 217
Domestic conundrums, 177–81
Domestic goddess celebration ritual, 179–80
Doubt, spell to banish, 116–17
Dream house, spell for finding, 138–39
Dreams (dream reading), 29–31
Drinks (drinking), 16, 65
    for attracting guys, 54
    for banishing love boxing matches, 150
    for breaking up, 200
    for dealing with ex, 120
    for dealing with his friends, 100
    for dealing with in-laws, 134
    for distinguishing good guys from bad, 62
    for domestic bliss, 181
    for first dates, 70
    for first sexual encounter, 78
    for flirting, 173
    for friends and boyfriend merger, 93
    for good sex, 107
    for living together, 144
    for mood swings, 192
    for proposals, 211
    for relationship's future, 165
    for relationships on the verge, 85
    for saying "I love you," 128
    for single girls, 43
    for vagabond hearts, 158
Drug use, 16

ℰ

Earl Grey tea, 100
Elements, defined, 217
Embarrassing sexual moments, 75
Emeralds, 210
Emotions. *See also* Blues; Happiness
    bath to revive, 170–71
    mood swings, 185–92
Energy. *See also* Negative energy; Positive energy
    centering when spell casting, 15
    clearing in magical space, 11–13
    spell for grounding, 187
Engagement, 203–11
Equinox, 34
Essential oils, 24–28. *See also specific oils*
    for attracting guys, 54
    for banishing love boxing matches, 150
    for breaking up, 200
    caution when using, iv
    for dealing with ex, 120
    for dealing with his friends, 100
    for dealing with in-laws, 134
    for distinguishing good guys from bad, 62
    for domestic bliss, 181
    for first dates, 70
    for first sexual encounter, 78
    for flirting, 173
    for friends and boyfriend merger, 93
    for good sex, 107
    for living together, 144
    for mood swings, 192
    for proposals, 211
    for relationship's future, 165
    for relationships on the verge, 85
    for saying "I love you," 128
    for single girls, 43
    for vagabond hearts, 158
Eucalyptus, 24
Evening primrose, 190
Evocations, defined, 217
Exercises (exercising), 17, 170–71
    for developing intuition, 28–29
    for hormonal mood swings, 188–90
    for space clearing, 11–13
Ex-girlfriends, 111–20

F

Familiar, defined, 217–18
Fascination contradiction spell, 154–55
Fast foods, 15, 191
Fatigue, 191
Fears about falling in love, spell to resolve, 127
Fennel, 144
Fertility, herbs for, 20
Feverfew, 62
Fights, silly, 147–50
Figs, 78, 106
Financial hassles, 138
    spell to banish, 140–41
Fire, 218
    future forecasting spell using, 155–56
First dates, 65–70
    after, 81–85
    ideas for where to go, 65–66
    safety spell for, 66–67
First sexual encounter, 73–78
    embarrassing moments, 75
    at home versus away, 74–75
    morning after, 77
    spells for, 75–77
Flirting, 51, 83, 169–73
    spells for, 51, 83–84
Food choices, 15–16, 190, 191
Found objects, 10, 23
Frankincense, 26–27, 54, 85
Friday, 20, 43, 70, 93, 107, 158
Friends (friendships)
    of boyfriend, 97–100
    charter of independence and commitment, 90–91
    meeting guys through, 47, 49–50
    new boyfriend and your, 89–93
    spell for true, 48–50
Full moon, 22
Future forecast spell, 155–56

G

Gabriel, 165
Gardens (gardening), 141–42
Gemini, moon in, 35
Getting over breakup spell, 198
Getting together spell, 205
Getting wise spell, 41–42
Ginger, 200
Girlfriends, 89–93
    ex's of boyfriend, 111–20
Glamour spell, 171–72

Glossary of magical terms, 215–21
Goddesses. *See specific goddesses*
Gold, 21, 100
Good guys, distinguishing bad from, 58–62
Gorgeous spell, 68–69
Granite, 181
Grapefruit, 43
Green, 21, 120
Green ribbons, 140–41
Green tea, 144
Grounding, 218
    crazy energy spell, 187
Guy magnet spell, 53
Guys. *See also* Boyfriend
    attracting and meeting, 47–54
    distinguishing good from bad, 57–62
    first date with, 65–70
    first sexual encounter with, 73–78

H

Happiness
    herbs for, 20
    signs to foretell future, 58–59
Hassles over petty things, charm to banish, 148–49
Healing, defined, 218
Health, herbs for, 20
Hecate, 192, 200
Helen of Troy, 54
Heliotrope, 158
Herbs, 20. *See also specific herbs*
    for banishing love boxing matches, 150
    for breaking up, 200
    for dealing with ex, 120
    for dealing with his friends, 100
    for dealing with in-laws, 134
    for distinguishing good guys from bad, 62
    for domestic bliss, 181
    for first dates, 70
    for first sexual encounter, 78
    for flirting, 173
    for friends and boyfriend merger, 93
    garden for, 141–42
    for good sex, 105, 107
    for living together, 144
    for mood swings, 192
    for proposals, 211
    for relationship's future, 165
    for relationships on the verge, 85
    for saying "I love you," 128
    for single girls, 43
    for vagabond hearts, 158

Holidays, 33–35
Home (house)
    banishing friends spell, 98
    housekeeping sins, 177–81
    living together. *See* Living together
    magical space at. *See* Magical space
    party ritual for blessing, 139–40
    safe and lovely spell for, 67–68
    spell for finding dream, 138–39
Honey, 106. *See also* Manuka honey
Hops, 106
Hormonal mood swings, 185–92
Hot prospects, 57–62
Hyacinth, 150

I

"I love you," 123–28
Imbolg, 34
Initiations, defined, 218–19
In-laws, 131–34
Intuition, 30, 205
    charm for, 124
    exercise for developing, 28–29
Invocations, defined, 219
Isis, 158
Ivory, 70

J

Jasmine, 28, 70, 107, 158
Jasmine tea, 200
Jasper, 85
Jealousy, 111
Joan of Arc, 134
Junk foods, 15, 191
Juno, 144

K

Karma, defined, 219
Keeping true love alive spell, 207
Kitt, Eartha, 78
Knowing spell, 205
Kwan Yin, 78, 134

L

Lapiz lazuli, 200
Laughter spell, 162–63
Lavender, 26, 134, 142, 150, 192

Law of threefold return, 14, 22–23
Lemon, 93, 165
Lemon verbena, 93, 134, 142, 178
Lennox, Annie, 134
Leo, moon in, 35
Letting go of the past, 42
Libra, moon in, 35
Light-heartedness laughter spell, 162–63
Lilac, 134, 181
Lime, 54, 85, 120
Living together, 137–44
    domestic conundrums, 177–81
Lonesome spell, 132
Losers, 58–62
Love, 6
    apple spell for, 163
    declaring your, 123–28
    detox spell for, 42
    falling flat, 147–50
    golden rules of, 9–10
    herbs for, 20
    revival spell for, 154
Love-frustration cure, 206
Lovemaking. *See* Sex
Love slumps, 153–58, 161–65
Loving home, magic charm for, 142–43
Loving yourself, 15, 17, 52

M

Magic. *See also* Spells
    glossary of terms, 215–21
    golden rules for, 9–10, 14–18
    how it works, 6
    how to use, 9–36
Magical gardening, 141–42
Magical powers, spell to reconnect, 125–26
Magical space, 9, 220
    creating and clearing, 10–13
Magnesium, 190
Magnolia, 140–41
Manuka honey, 106, 150, 192
Marjoram, 43
Marriage, 203–11
    spell for, 208–9
Mead, 107
Meditation, 17, 219. *See also* Color breathing
Meeting great guys, 47–54
Meeting parents, 131–34
Men. *See* Guys
Minerva, 43
Mint, 173

Mr. Maybe, 81, 89
Mr. Right versus Mr. Wrong, 57–62
    spell to know if he's, 81–82
Mr. Walking Wounded, 58, 61
Mr. Wow, 61
Monday, 19
Money hassles, 138
    spell to banish, 140–41
Monroe, Marilyn, 43, 93
Mood swings, 185–92
Moon (moon magic), 21–22, 35–36, 219
Moonstone, 128
Morning after, 77
Movie dates, 65
Moving in together, 137–44
Moving on spell, 198
Muscle cramps, 190
Myrrh, 27

N

Necromancy, defined, 219
Negative energy (attitude), 9–10, 15, 42
    spell to banish, 117
Neighbors, hassles with, 142
Neroli, 25
New moon, 22
Newton-John, Olivia, 43
No money hassles spell, 140–41
Nurturing yourself, 15–16

O

Occult, defined, 219–20
Ocean pebbles, 120
O'Hara, Scarlett, 85
Oils. *See* Essential oils
Onions, peel away anger spell with, 133
Opals, 144
Orange (color), 21, 54
Out-laws, 131–34
Oysters, 106

P

Palmarosa, 120
Parents, meeting his, 131–34
Passion. *See* First sexual encounter; Sex
Passionate first night spell, 75–76
Past, release from, 42
Patchouli, 43, 173

Peach nectar, 128
Pearls, 134
Peel away anger spell, 133
Pelvic thrusts, 189–90
Pennyroyal, 142
Pentagrams, defined, 220
Pernod, 173
Persephone, 107, 154
Personal boundaries, 147–50
Perspective on meeting guys, 5, 41
Pick-me-up spell, 132
Picnic dates, 65
Pink, 21, 43, 85, 107, 206
Pink diamonds, 210
Pisces, moon in, 36
Planetary days, defined, 220
PMS, 185–92
Positive energy (attitude), 9–10, 14, 15, 32
Post-honeymoon period, 153–58, 161–65, 169–73
Prayers, 32
Precious stones. *See* Stones; *and specific stones*
Priapus, 106
Proposals, 203–11
Prosperity, herbs for, 20
Protection
    herbs for, 20
    spell against stalkers, 115–16
Psyche, 173
Purple, 21
Purple cabbage, 132

Q

Quarters, defined, 220
Quartz, 62. *See also* Rose quartz
Quiz, sex chemistry, 104–5

R

Red, 21, 85, 107
Red wine, 93, 107
Rekindling romance, 153–58, 169–73
Relationship angst spell, 82
Relationships
    ambiguity and future of, 161–65
    being on the verge, 81–85
    breaking up, 195–200
    cheating, 111–20
    marriage, 203–11
    rekindling, 153–58, 169–73
    saying "I love you," 123–28

Responsibility, for spell casting, 14
Rhodonite, 54
Rituals, defined, 220
Roadblocks to meeting boyfriend, 39–40
Rock rose, 181
Romance body lotion, 156–57
Rose, 26, 85, 107, 150, 211
Rose geranium, 24–25, 192
Rosemary, 25, 93
Rose quartz, 43, 91, 150
Rosewood, 43, 128
Rubies, 107, 150, 158, 209
Rules for spell casting, 9–10, 14–18
Russell, Jane, 93

S

Sacred space, 9, 220
    creating and clearing, 10–13
Safe home spell, 67–68
Safety on dates spell, 66–67
Sagittarius, moon in, 35
St. John's wort, 142
Samhain, 34–35
Sandalwood, 12, 27, 200
Sapphires, 210
Saturday, 20, 78, 120, 150, 165, 181
Saying "I love you," 123–28
Scarlet, 107, 158
Scorpio, moon in, 35
Scrying, defined, 220
Seductress spell, 76–77
Seinfeld, Jerry, 195–96
Selene, 85
Self-esteem, 48, 52, 169. *See also* Loving yourself
    beautiful self spell for, 117
Semillon, 70
Serotonin, 16
Sex, 103–7. *See also* First sexual encounter
    aphrodisiacs, 105–6
    cheating with ex, 111–20
    chemistry quiz, 104–5
    at different times, 207–8
    rekindling romance, 153–58, 169–73
Silver, 54, 134, 173
Silver ribbon, 66–67
Sleep, importance of, 17
Smoking, 18
Smudge sticks, 117
Soul mate spellpaper, 118–19
Sowilo, 188
Special days of the year, for spell casting, 33–35

Spells (spell casting), 9–36. *See also specific spells*
    astrology for, 35–36
    four easy steps for, 28–34
    golden rules for, 9–10, 14–18
    how they work, 6
    items required for, 23–28
    magical correspondences, 19–23
    magical space for, 10–13
    special days of the year for, 33–35
    storing and re-energizing, 19
Spirits, 12
Spring water, 62
Stalking (stalkers), 115–16
Star spell, for dream house, 138–39
Stewart, Martha, 181
Stones, 209–10. *See also specific stones*
    for attracting guys, 54
    for banishing love boxing matches, 150
    for breaking up, 200
    for dealing with ex, 120
    for dealing with his friends, 100
    for dealing with in-laws, 134
    for distinguishing good guys from bad, 62
    for domestic bliss, 181
    for first dates, 70
    for first sexual encounter, 78
    for flirting, 173
    for friends and boyfriend merger, 93
    for good sex, 107
    for living together, 144
    for mood swings, 192
    for proposals, 211
    for relationship's future, 165
    for relationships on the verge, 85
    for saying "I love you," 128
    for single girls, 43
    for vagabond hearts, 158
Strawberries, 164
Stress, 15
Sunday, 19, 78, 85, 134, 144, 211
Sunrises, 178–79
Sunsets, 178–79
Superstitions, 179

T

Talismans, 220–21
    for resisting bad guys, 60
Tangerine, 144
Tarot cards, 28, 148–49
Taurus, moon in, 35
Taylor, Elizabeth, 192

Tea
- chai, 165
- chamomile, 150
- Earl Grey, 100
- green, 144
- jasmine, 200

Tea tree oil, 181
Temples, defined, 221
Thaumaturgy, defined, 221
Threefold law, 14, 22–23
Thursday, 20
Tibetan bells, 12–13
Tiger's eye stone, 116
Toilet seats, 177, 179, 181
Tomatoes, 106
Topaz, 173, 210
Tree reading, 140–41
True friendship spell, 48–50
True romance body lotion, 156–57
True romance spell, 124–25
Truffles, 106
Trust (trusting), 116–17
- in your inner self, 17

Truth spell, 116–17
Tuesday, 19–20, 62, 100, 128, 200
Turquoise, 21, 173

U

Uncasting, defined, 221
Unfair tactics spell, 98–99
Uplift spell, 132

V

Valerian, 211
Vanilla, 207
Venus, 210
Violet, 21
Virginity, 73
Virgo, moon in, 35
Visualizations, 18, 51, 221
Vitamin B foods, 190, 191
Vivian, 120
Vodka, 78

W

Waning moon, 22
Wards, defined, 221
Water retention, 190
Waxing moon, 22
Wedding rings, 208–9
Wednesday, 20, 54, 170, 173
White, 20, 85, 211
Wicca, defined, 221
Widdershins, defined, 221
Witch hazel, 100

X

Xena, 93, 134

Y

Yellow, 21
Ylang ylang, 26, 78, 107

Z

Zenith, defined, 221

Acknowledgments

Big thankyous and hand-hurting applause to: all of my (girl and boy) friends who've encouraged me—but especially the lovely Jo Mitchell; to my Mum and Dad, and brother Mark, for loving me and teaching me about having an open mind; to all my work friends, but especially the hilarious Lucy Macken and the inspiring Melinda Pearson; to Sasha Mackie, for the epiphany that was Los Angeles; to Kate Pollard for being a clever, clever editor and a sister shoe-obsessive; to Helen Littleton for her steadfast support and astute analysis of where celebrity couples really do go wrong; to Annette Hughes for getting it—effortlessly; and to Stephen, for honey toast in bed and always believing in me enough to wonder what I was worrying about, anyway. And to Thomasina, because she is my darling.

Sheryn George lives in Sydney with her husband, her daughter, his labradoodle, and her cat. She is Associate Editor—Features of *The Sunday Telegraph*.